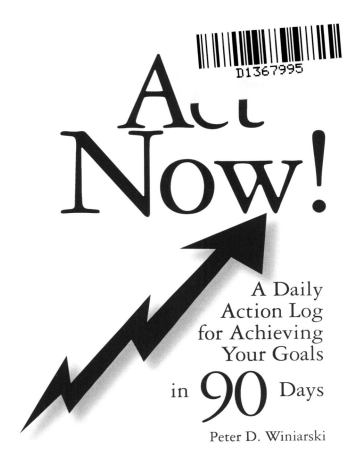

Act Now!

A Daily Action Log for Achieving Your Goals in 90 Days

Peter D. Winiarski

Visit www.DailyActionLog.com for free access
to tools and resources that compliment this book.

ISBN: 098268651X
ISBN 13: 9780982686515

Library of Congress Control Number: 2011962973
CreateSpace, North Charleston, SC

About Win Publishing

Win Publishing, LLC publishes books that help you, well...win! Of course, winning isn't everything, and we believe how you play the game matters a lot, too.

You decide if you're looking to improve your business, career, financial situation, relationships, health and fitness, overall happiness, or something else about yourself. Resources from Win Publishing can help you.

We also have a children's book division, N&N Publishing. Here you'll find inspirational and fun children's books for the amazing kids in your life.

For more information about Win Publishing, LLC, or to be published by us, visit www.WinPublishingLLC.com.

Note to eBook Readers

Hi, eBook reader!

In addition to great content to help you understand how to use all three types of action to achieve each of your goals, there are Daily Action Log pages to help you stay on track. You might be wondering, "How can I use the log sheets in an eBook?" We have a solution.

We have posted copies of the log sheets and all other forms contained in the book at www.DailyActionLog.com. You can download the forms there! The forms and other information will be updated on this web page, so come back often.

Enjoy!

Pete O. Winiarski

Pete

Praise for Act Now!

"When I began to use Act Now! *I saw a shift in my results right away. It forced me to focus each day on what was critical in reaching my goals. After 3 weeks of use (normally 5 minutes per day) I knew that I needed to order copies for my management team, family, and friends so they could benefit, too."*

- Alan Nathan, CPA, Managing Member
of Nathan Accounting Group

"Pete Winiarski has applied his adept business expertise to create a "success guaranteed" plan for you. His clear and direct instruction will definitely inspire you to action!"

- Dr. Deborah Sandella, Award Winning Author,
Founder and CEO of the RIM Institute

"Pete Winiarski is a truly powerful leader, incredible mentor, and a very gifted teacher. He is committed to studying the psychology of success and teaching only the best practices that WORK. If you're ready to dramatically accelerate your results in the next 90 days, implement Pete's strategies now. Your life will never be the same."

- Sean Smith, Founder MVP Success Systems

"The most critical element in Leadership and Leadership Development is making things happen. In order to get what we want we need to stay focused and motivated for significant periods of time and learn from our experiences. Pete Winiarski brings us a simple tool with Act Now! *that will help you do just that."*

- Jaroslav Průša, Leadership Development
Trainer & Executive Coach

"If you're serious about achieving your goals then look no further! Act Now! *will guide you down the path."*

    - Kathryn Hanford, Vice President, Business
           Process Integration, Hasbro, Inc.

*"*Act Now! *provides a great approach for those who have a natural bent towards setting goals and breaking them down into more manageable pieces. It makes the process for getting into action to achieve your goals rather easy and straight-forward."*

    - Chris Goralski, CEO of SynGas Technology, LLC

"Brilliant. Simple. Powerful. This book delivers."

    - Marilyn Suttle, Author and CEO of
           Suttle Enterprises

*"*Act Now! *demystifies the process of setting and reaching your goals by breaking down your goals into manageable steps that you control.* Act Now! *can help put you on the road to success."*

    - Leland Brant, Co-owner, The Research Department

"Both a compilation of proven success tips and insightful steps toward making them work for you. A simple and accurate way to move forward in defining the aspirations of the reader. This book can change your life."

    - Bruce H. Stanger, Esq., Stanger & Arnold, LLC
           Attorney at Law

"If you are looking to upgrade your results and looking to create what you want out of your life, then Act Now! *is your book. Pete Winiarski uses true methods that are simple, clear, mind opening, and fun! Since implementing the* Act Now! *methodology, my business has improved, my playtime has increased, my relationships are better…I'm living the balanced and rewarding life I love to live. If you want similar results to create the life you're longing for, then Pete Winiarski's* Act Now! *is a must!"*

- Kym Belden, Founder and Owner of Physical Culture,
a Fitness and Sports Performance Company
and Co-author of the book *Power to Change*

*"*Act Now! *is totally aligned with the "Manifesting for Non-Gurus" approach I teach. It is a great way to stay focused, in action, and quickly accomplish amazing results. Read it now, follow the approach for the next 90 days, and be ready to celebrate having reached your goals!"*

Robert MacPhee, Speaker, Success Coach
Author of *Manifesting for Non- Gurus*

"I've known Pete Winiarski and his work for a long time, and this book aligns well with his fun and impactful style of helping people achieve at the next level. Act Now! *is a great resource to help you hit your personal goals and to focus your team members on hitting the team goals. It is easy to see how following this methodology can shift your company's culture to be more proactive and action oriented."*

- Glenn Munshaw, EVP Operations
Alloy Polymers

"Why make something harder than it has to be? In Act Now! *Pete Winiarski has given the reader easy to understand, and more importantly, easy to follow and use ideas, tips, and strategies to help them achieve their goals. This book is a must for anyone wanting to achieve their goals."*

- Sharon Worsley, CEO of Sharon
Worsley International

If you are looking for the quickest way to achieve results that road to success is right here! In this deceivingly simple book is a concise strategy to make your next 90 days change your life. Author and consultant Pete Winiarski has trained with the best and it shows. His years of experience and his straightforward, fun approach make this book accessible to everyone!"

Holly Carnes, CEO/CFO, MOM, and Professional Coach,
Carnes Professional Coaching

Act Now! *makes it easy for companies to take action and execute toward strategic goals. Beyond just having written goals and action plans, this book makes it clear about the actions which need to take place each day toward achieving goals and getting better results. I'm making sure my team understands how to do this. If you want your team to maximize its performance then you should, too*

~ John Uliano, Director Operations – Americas,
HID Global

Act Now! *is good for you… if you want to accelerate your personal journey, read this; don't delay. Act now!*

~ Walt Hampton, Speaker, Coach, Best-selling
Author of *Journeys on the Edge: Living a Life That Matters*

Table of Contents

Foreword

I've been teaching the Success Principles for over thirty years, and every year thousands of people go through my private and public seminars and workshops—business leaders of large corporations, entrepreneurs, professional athletes, stay-at-home moms—anyone who wants to change their results and enjoy new levels of success. One of the things I strongly recommend is building daily routines for many of the principles I teach.

I've personally practiced these principles by creating my own daily routines and have seen tremendous results in my relationships, my business, and my personal finances. Truly, I've experienced amazing results in all the areas of my life, and these principles are a core reason why.

While many of my students have achieved fantastic goals, other people who set goals still struggle to achieve them, and from observing what works, I realize that it's what we do on a day-to-day basis that propels us to reach our goals.

If you're one of those people who sometimes still struggles to achieve your goals, then pay close attention. Maybe you get excited about the goals you just set, but you lose momentum after a while. Maybe you've never set goals and don't know how to start. Maybe you're just not yet familiar with the wide array of techniques to help you know what actions to take on a daily basis that *will* accelerate your results. I'm also willing to bet you have not yet set up the daily routines that will lock in the benefits of your efforts.

My friend Pete Winiarski is a business leader who understands these Success Principles well. He assists at my workshops, he has graduated from my elite Train the Trainer program, he runs his own workshops and teaches these principles to his clients, and he utilizes them in his own life and business. In fact, *Act Now!* grew out of techniques he created for himself to help him take action every day toward his goals.

Act Now! is totally aligned with the lessons I teach in my workshops. The three short chapters are quick to read and provide an excellent overview of what Pete calls the three types of action: planned actions, daily habits, and inspired actions. I agree with Pete that all three types of action are important. French writer Antoine de Saint-Exupery said, "A goal without a plan is just a wish." His statement captures the essence of planned actions, as it's important that you give deliberate thought about the steps you will take to reach your goals. Daily habits include the application of many Success Principles that are outlined clearly within this book that, when made a disciplined part of your daily routine, will accelerate your goal achievement. Last, inspired actions are those actions we take based on the inspirational ideas and intuitive insights that are evoked by those daily habits we form.

I've been true to all three types of action and have been rewarded handsomely. I write action steps for my goals and take planned action daily. I practice a number of daily habits such as saying affirmations, visualizing my goals as already complete, releasing negative emotions, practicing gratitude, and meditating. As a result, I regularly receive intuitive insights, or "hits," and I am sure to immediately take inspired action when I do. In fact, the title of *Chicken Soup for the Soul* came from taking inspired action after meditating. The Chicken Soup series has now reportedly sold over five hundred million copies in forty-seven languages because of that action.

You'll find that the Daily Action Log pages within *Act Now!* are unique, and they create a simple method for engaging in all three types of action, every day. They also provide you with feedback about your progress in using the methodology described in the book, and you will easily know where you need to make adjustments.

Now, rather than lose momentum after setting your goals, you can use this book to help guide you and keep you on track. If you are a business leader, you can share this methodology with your team to help create an action-oriented culture as they continually set and achieve their goals. You can also use this methodology with your friends and family members, or accountability partners and mastermind team members, as a common format to support each other on your goal-achievement journeys.

Act Now! will make your journey much easier. Pete masterfully presents these powerful principles in a clear, simple way. His writing style will make you feel comfortable trying out these methods, and before you know it, you will have created enormous momentum toward your next ninety-day goals.

Apply the principles in *Act Now!* and use the Daily Action Log for your current and future goals. You will be amazed at the results that will come to you when you do!

Jack Canfield

Best-selling author of
The Success Principles,
Chicken Soup for the Soul,
The Power of Focus,
and many other titles

The Circle That Will Change Your Results™

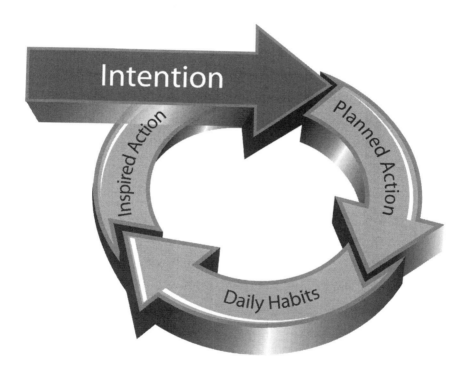

Introduction

Welcome to *Act Now! A Daily Action Log for Achieving Your Goals in 90 Days*. This book will help you create the results you want by taking action on your goals.

I have personally achieved so much across all areas of my life using some simple processes and methods to help me meet the goals I've set for myself. Many people have asked me what I do and want to know the best way for them to get similar great results. The answer is simple, and I'm sharing what I do in this book. You can follow the effortless steps outlined within and find that you will achieve your goals faster, too.

In *Act Now!* I describe the basics of taking daily action toward your most important goals and provide a ninety-day Daily Action Log to keep you on track to achieve those goals. After the first ninety days, you'll find that this book is a useful tool that you'll want to use for all your goals every ninety days.

You may be wondering, "Why a log book?" I have found that people like to have an easy-to-follow structure to help keep them on track. This Daily Action Log is designed with some of the best principles of goal achievement in mind, and it incorporates them into a fun way to help you keep score. I have also found that when I have had someone or something to help me set goals and keep my commitments, such as a coach or a daily log book, I have made progress much faster than when I didn't have these tools in place.

My first memorable experience with a log book was for exercising during 1999, when I was training for my first marathon. I had a coach, a running team, a good pair of sneakers, and my log book. The coach gave me input on the goals to set and the plans to execute (our workout schedule), and he had lots of advice and answers to my questions. The running team created a community of like-minded goal achievers who would happily run between ten and twenty-six miles on the weekend together and share encouragement, social activities, and the travel experience to the marathon locations. The sneakers were important tools of the trade to achieve my goal. Last, I had my log book.

My marathon log book chronicled my miles, the routes, how I felt during the run. It gave me a record of my food, my energy level, my speed, and my progress toward my goals. By checking the log book, I could quickly determine if I was on track or off track. The log book provided motivation toward reaching my goal that was six months away when I started my plan. I loved my log book and I credit using it as a major contributor toward reaching that goal and completing my first marathon.

Perhaps you've also had some experiences with daily journals or log books. They are certainly popular for athletics like running a marathon, and I've used them for other training (such as weight lifting, my first triathlon, etc.) and for resizing my body to reach my ideal body weight by monitoring both food and exercise. If a daily log book can be useful to hit athletic and fitness goals, why not goals in other areas of my life, too?

I have been a goal setter for years. I realized there were times when I absolutely blew away my goals, and other times when I struggled and maybe didn't meet them. I looked for patterns, and I discovered three things. First, when I've achieved the most, I noticed that I followed some great daily habits. Second, I had an action plan for my goal and did something toward reaching that goal every day. Third, I would frequently get "intuitive hits"—ideas or insights. If I quickly followed through on them, I would find my progress surged ahead.

This is the foundation of what I call the three types of action:

1. Daily habits

2. Planned actions

3. Inspired actions

Unknown to me at the time, these habits engage the Science of Success and Goal Achievement Theory from the perspectives of both biology and quantum physics. My brain's reticular activating system (RAS), the law of attraction, and other universal truths kicked into gear even though I was unaware that they existed. I'll describe more of the Science of Success throughout chapter 2.

This was exciting for me to discover, as it tied together the Goal Achievement Theory and the Science of Success with the daily practice that enables goal achievement. By following a few simple habits, you can accelerate your results tremendously.

Here are some of the daily habits that I've followed that have helped me blow away my goals:

- Holding a clear intention for the day
- Visualizing my goals and saying affirmations
- Expressing appreciation and gratitude
- Meditating and journaling
- Reading
- Exercising
- "Letting Go" of the emotional charge attached to issues or events
- Taking specific, planned action steps for the day
- Reviewing my progress—How did I do today? Where can I improve?

Maybe the daily habits on this list are not a surprise to you. Even if not, let me challenge you—do you follow them every day? Even though I know these things are good to do every day, I admit that I don't always follow every one of these habits. Why not? Like you, I'm busy and get caught up in being, well…too busy.

But isn't that the point? These habits are simple daily disciplines that can compress the amount of time it takes to achieve your goals! So, when you're "too busy," it's the perfect time to invest a few minutes of your day to put these concepts into practice.

The planned action steps for the day would follow my action plan. And, if I paid attention to my intuition, I would often get intuitive guidance—ideas to pursue. I call following through on these ideas taking inspired action.

I know that when I follow these daily habits, the planned actions, and any inspired action that pops into my consciousness, I tend to experience great results more quickly. I expect the same will be true for you, too.

To make it easy for you (and me) to accelerate your results using these principles, I designed a tracking tool to use every day. After multiple iterations, I came up with a fun way for you to get into action and make your most important goals a reality. The result is this Daily Action Log.

It incorporates daily habits, planned actions, and inspired actions. It also creates a simple way for you to keep score—notice that the times when your daily score is higher, you are making more progress in a way that feels more effortless, and which daily habits help you the most.

This book is organized into three short chapters and then the Daily Action Log. In chapter 1, "Define Your Goals," I lead you through a few simple exercises so you can decide what goals you want to focus on for your next ninety-day period. In chapter 2, "The Basics of Daily Actions," I describe the three types of action in more detail. This chapter lays a foundation for you so that you understand how to utilize all three types of action for any goal you set. In chapter 3, "How to Use This Daily Action Log," I describe the layout of the Daily Action Log and share some tips to help you get the most out of using it to achieve your goals in ninety days.

Watch for this symbol indicating "Your Action," which describes actions that I suggest you take right away.

The Daily Action Log section comes next with thirteen weeks of log pages, enough for you to cover the next ninety days.

You Will Get Amazing Results

Whether you are planning to use *Act Now!* to achieve all your personal goals or share it with your team to drive progress toward your business goals, you'll find that you get amazing results. I believe you will far exceed your previous progress if you use this Daily Action Log versus the methods you've used before. The Daily Action Log will benefit you in the following ways:

- You will be more focused on the goals you really want to achieve, now.

- You will learn to use all three types of action rather than just one (or none!), which means you'll get there faster.

- You will engage the Science of Success and leverage biology and quantum physics to accelerate your results.

- You will learn some powerful principles and apply them with ease.

- Last but not least, you will have fun!

Now, let's get started!

Special Note to Business Leaders

Dear Business Leader,

As a business leader, you certainly want great results for yourself. You also have the added desire to deliver great results for your business. This book and the Daily Action Log method it teaches can help you achieve the results you seek.

Imagine the action-oriented culture you will create for your team if your team members all learned this method and used the Daily Action Log with you. You will create a common language and enhance teamwork by going through the process together. You can also make a game of the scoring if you think your team would respond well to that added dimension. If you already use accountability partners or mastermind teams (see chapter 2), the Daily Action Log augments this process well, too.

As a business leader myself in corporate roles and now of my own company, Win Enterprises, LLC, I understand how important it is to get everyone aligned and focused on the most important goals. We've created the Win Holistic Transformation Model™ to help you and your team achieve and sustain transformational results for your business.

The core elements of Win Holistic Transformation Model™ help drive you toward the results you seek. They also help shape your culture to one that assures success over the long term. This culture's attributes include being action-oriented. Look at the resources on www.WinEnterprisesLLC.com for a full description of the Win Holistic Transformation Model™.

While it's true that I created *Act Now!* initially as a method for individual use, I quickly realized the power of extending it to all members of a management team and their subsequent teams. *Act Now!* and the Daily Action Log will help you as a business leader to achieve your personal goals. It will also support your team members to achieve their goals and, as a result, develop an action-oriented culture that will help make you unstoppable.

 Watch for this symbol throughout the book. It indicates additional notes that apply to business leaders.

I hope you and your whole team enjoy using this book and the Daily Action Log process.

Best regards,

Pete

CHAPTER 1

Define Your Goals

If you already have a written list of your current goals, good for you! In reviewing 110 studies conducted between 1969 and 1980, Edwin A. Locke discovered that setting specific and challenging goals, as opposed to setting easy goals or not setting goals at all, led to higher performance 90 percent of the time. According to a study at Dominican University, writing your goals down will make you 42.1 percent more apt to achieve them than you were before you put them on paper.[1]

If you don't have a current list of goals, or perhaps you want to refresh your list, the exercises in this chapter will help you. You will end up with a clear set of goals that you will achieve during the next ninety days using the Daily Action Log.

In this chapter, I'll talk about the basics of goal setting then get into your specific goals for the next ninety days. Doing these goal-setting exercises now, before we get into the details about the three types of action in chapter 2 and how to use this Daily Action Log in chapter 3, will help you immediately personalize the content in this book.

Basics of Goal Setting

Before we nail down your specific goals, let's briefly talk about goal setting. You may have heard the acronym SMART goals. SMART stands for: Specific, Measurable, Achievable, Relevant, and Time-bound. Let me describe what each means.

- Specific—Eliminate any vague language and create clarity in your mind. Rather than "lose weight," you want to "weigh 178 pounds." Rather than "improve net income," you will "earn a net income of $5,312,000." Use a specific number where possible.

- Measurable—Your goal must be something that can be measured and observed by someone else. To measure if you do indeed weigh 178 pounds, you can step on a scale and read the number. To measure your net income, you can look at your income statement to see $5,312,000.

- Achievable—Your goal must be something that you believe you can achieve. Consider whether or not other people have done what you say you want to do. If to hit your weight goal of 178 pounds you need to lose twenty pounds in thirteen weeks, you can indeed achieve this, as 1) other people have achieved similar reductions and 2) it falls within nutritional guidelines to safely lose one to two pounds of fat per week. Your task here is to make sure you believe the goal is possible for you to achieve, so get in touch with what you believe. Is $5.3 million net income achievable, or is it twice as much as you would expect even if everything went perfectly?

- Relevant—This means the goal is relevant to you and that you care about it. If you are resistant about your goal because you haven't bought into it, you probably won't achieve it.

- Time-bound—Your goal has a due date. The due date says you're serious about achieving that goal and will do what is possible to get there—you'll put in your best effort.

You'll notice from the above guidelines that your goals are personal to you. If you don't believe you can achieve it, don't care about it, or don't want it in the first place, you simply won't put in the effort to achieve that goal. Periodically scrutinize your list of goals and make sure they are indeed right for you. I'll lead you through a goal-setting exercise shortly so you can write goals for the next ninety days or review your current list.

Here are some examples of goals:

- By July 31, 2013, I will weigh 178 pounds.

- By November 1, 2013, I will have the beta test complete for the ABC web application and have the marketing package ready for new customers.

- By December 31, 2013, I will improve the productivity of my division by 15 percent from 1.00 to 1.15.

- By December 31, 2013, I will ensure 100 percent of my team members complete the Goal Accelerator audio program.

- By December 31, 2013, my team will have a net income of $5,312,000 for this fiscal year.

- By September 30, 2014, I will complete the first draft of my next book.

- By March 31, 2014, I will have scheduled that summer's vacation for my family and me to enjoy in Kennebunk, Maine.

- By August 31, 2014, I will complete an Olympic distance triathlon.

Now, there is something called "high intention/low attachment" that I want you to practice. My paradoxical advice here is to go after your goal with the full intention of achieving it on time, but do not measure your worth as a person based on the result. Stuff sometimes happens outside our control that we don't quite understand at the time, but realize later it somehow helped us. The important thing is that you give yourself credit for effort and intention. You can always revise your goals as the situation changes.

Here's an interesting concept for you to consider from my friend Jim Bunch, founder of the Ultimate Game of Life (for more information see www.DailyActionLog.com). Jim says we tend to overestimate what we can accomplish in the short term, but underestimate what we can accomplish in the long term. This implies that we will typically have super-ambitious short-term goals (e.g., daily, weekly, monthly). We may not hit them all, but the cumulative impact will equate to a lot of long term progress and great results if we keep at it.

So keep at it! Use the Daily Action Log every day and reap the rewards!

Setting Your Goals

As you decide what you will achieve in the next ninety days, consider these points:

- What is your current workload and available capacity? For example, if you have a heavy travel schedule coming up, you may want to cut back a bit on your expectations.

- Think of how many different goals you want to take on. If you take on more goals, you'll be able to make some progress across them all, but less progress on any one goal than if you decide to take on fewer goals. If it's critical to get one of your goals to completion on time or early, take on fewer goals.

- Always add some amount of stretch to your goals. If you can reasonably expect to get up to thirty, shoot for thirty-five or forty. If you can reasonably expect to get down to 180, shoot for 170. Get the idea?

The Goal-Setting Exercises

Start by listing any longer-term goals you already have. By "longer term" I mean beyond the next ninety days. Many goal setters do an annual exercise to set goals for the year. Some people list 101 goals they want to achieve and some have time frames well beyond the next year.

If you don't have an existing list, that's okay, too. You can create one now using the Twelve-Month Goals worksheet on page 13.

> ## Note to Business Leaders: Goals Exercises
>
> As a business leader, you can achieve more if your whole team becomes great goal achievers. The methods in this Daily Action Log can be used for any goal.
>
> Notice that the five categories in the goal-setting exercises represent a whole person's interests, not just business goals. You can expect to see your business results improve even if your team uses this process to work on personal goals. There are three reasons for this:
>
> - *First, goal achievement is a skill.* As your team learns to set goals, take all three types of action as described in chapter 2, and achieve great results in one area of their life, the experience translates to other areas, including your business.
>
> - *Second, your team members have lives both inside and outside work.* If you can help them become fulfilled in all areas of their life, their self-esteem and total contentment will go up. This makes them better team members at work.
>
> - *Third, having your whole team go through the experience of setting goals, taking action, and achieving great results will create a shared experience.* You can expect this to aid in team cohesiveness and make the team more productive.
>
> Nonetheless, you can use this book only for work-related goals if you choose.

Twelve-Month Goals

Take a moment and think of the next year. What do you want to accomplish in the next twelve months? Consider these five categories: financial, business/career, health/fitness, relationships, and overall happiness. (In his Breakthrough to Success seminar, Jack Canfield uses seven categories: financial, business/career, relationships, health/fitness, fun time and recreation, personal, and contribution and legacy. Use whatever framework helps you decide on your goals.)

Here is a brief description of each goal category:

- Financial—Think of your income, net worth, debt, cash flow, bank account balance, and anything having to do with money.

- Business/career—Think of your job if you work for someone else, or your business if you work for yourself. Consider where you want to be in a year—what are you doing, where, with whom?

- Health/fitness—These goals are about your body's looks, abilities, and overall performance. They can include improving your health, losing weight, and any activities you want to complete (like running five miles, competing in a triathlon, biking twenty-five miles from your house to your sister's house, hiking the Appalachian Trail, etc.).

- Relationships—As relationships include any people with whom you interact, you can think of your family, friends, boss or coworkers, clients, customers, suppliers, neighbors, or anyone else you care to know or get along with better.

- Overall happiness—This is the category for goals personal to you, like buying your dream house or dream car; taking trips; completing personal development programs; reading books; learning new skills (e.g., golf, piano, speaking French); practicing yoga, meditation, or qigong; or anything that would give you a sense of personal satisfaction and joy.

Your Action—Twelve-Month Goals

Use the Twelve-Month Goals worksheet on page 13 to write your goals for the next twelve months. Go ahead and write down at least two goals that you will achieve in the next twelve months in each of the five categories. You can have more if you want, just be sure to have something in each category.

You can also download a blank copy of this worksheet at www.DailyActionLog.com.

Note to Business Leaders

You might already have a process by which you define your goals annually. Strategic Goal Deployment™ (SGD™) is the method I teach my business clients. This includes cascading the goals through your organization, defining metrics and monthly targets, and creating action plans for each metric. The SGD™ output is easily adapted for use with the Daily Action Log.

See Win Enterprises, LLC, on our Resources page at www. DailyActionLog.com for more information.

Ninety-Day Goals

You now need to decide on your goals for the next ninety days. Considering the twelve-month goals you just wrote, write the goals that will be your focus for the next ninety days and for the duration of this Daily Action Log.

With your twelve-month goals in front of you, be specific about the next ninety days and decide how much you will achieve. Will you focus heavily on just a few of your longer-term goals, drive them closer to completion, and then select a different set of goals for the subsequent ninety-day period? Will you work on all your goals equally?

As ninety days is essentially 25 percent of the year, you could take your annual goals and strive to get 25 percent of the way there. However, you will likely have more success if you are more aggressive and attempt to achieve 30 to 35 percent of your annual goals in the next ninety days.

For those of you who have already written goals for the year and have created action plans for each goal, these action plans might help you set your ninety-day goals. What do your action plans suggest you should be doing over the next thirteen weeks? Set your goals accordingly, with some stretch to complete them ahead of schedule.

Your Action—Ninety-Day Goals

Refer to your list of twelve-month goals and use the Ninety-Day Goals worksheet on page 14 to write your goals for the next ninety days. You can also download a blank copy of this worksheet at www.DailyActionLog.com.

Note to Business Leaders

If you use Strategic Goal Deployment™, you can use the targets for three months out that you defined in the target-setting section for each of your metrics.

Required Weekly Progress Rate

Now that you have defined your ninety-day goals, you have 12.85 weeks to achieve them. How much do you have to complete each week in order to be on time? It helps to know this as you plan your actions. For each of your goals, calculate your required weekly progress rate.

Start by evaluating your starting point, or where you are right now. Compare that to your goal and figure out what the gap is. Take that gap and divide by twelve weeks (because dividing by thirteen weeks would cause you to miss your goal by a couple days, so let's finish early). This is the rate you need to work at steadily over the next ninety days in order to achieve your goal on time.

For example, if you weigh 190 pounds today and your ninety-day goal is to reach 178 pounds, you have a gap of twelve pounds. Divide the gap of twelve pounds by twelve weeks and you will need to drop one pound per week. That's your required weekly progress rate.

If your goal is to grow the revenue of new products to $18 million in this quarter, that is a weekly progress rate of $1.5 million.

It's possible that not all your goals are numerical, or that they require a lot of work leading up to one big event that, when finished, your goal is achieved. If that's the case, appreciate the spirit of this exercise, which is to provide a sense of what you need to accomplish on a weekly basis. This will guide you when you create your action plan to ensure you achieve your goals.

For example, if your ninety-day goal is to take your draft manuscript and self-publish it as a completed book, you might review your action plan and set milestones through the thirteen weeks such as:

Week 1: Select publisher

Week 2: Understand submission requirements

Week 3: Submit manuscript

Week 4: Discuss cover design concepts

Week 5: Review publisher recommendations

Week 6: Discuss interior concepts

Week 7: Submit manuscript revisions

Week 8: Confirm all edits are correct

Week 9: Finalize manuscript

Your Action—Required Weekly Progress Rate

For each of your ninety-day goals

1. Evaluate your starting point—where you are right now;

2. Identify the gap from where you are to your ninety-day goal;

3. Calculate your required weekly rate by dividing the gap by twelve weeks; and

4. Use this rate to plan your weekly goals.

Use the Required Weekly Progress Rate worksheet on page 15 to calculate your required weekly progress rate for one of your goals. You can also download a blank copy of this worksheet at www.DailyActionLog.com. Use this information as you create your action plans and decide on your goals each week.

Action Plans

An action plan is simply a list of the actions you plan to take to achieve your goal. Based on what you know at the time you set the goal, define the steps that must be taken, by whom (they are not always to be done by you), and by when. If you can get a clear idea on paper of what it will take to hit your goals, you can begin to take those steps according to your plan.

While we don't always know everything we will do in great detail, we should have a good idea how we'll get started. An action plan for a ninety-day goal may be rather detailed for the first month and more general for the second and third months, as it can be difficult to predict exact steps and timing that far in advance.

An action plan is a live document, which means that as you learn more you can make edits to your action plans. You can edit the timing if you're ahead or behind schedule. You can add new steps as you discover more detail about what you'll need to do to meet your goal. You can get help and assign other people to steps on your action plans.

I suggest you create an action plan for each of your goals. It may require some research to create your action plan but at least start with what you know now. You can add to it as you gain clarity about what you'll need to do to achieve your goal.

Your Action—Action Plans

Create an action plan for each of your goals. Consider what it will take to achieve that goal and write down the steps. Decide the date by which you will complete each step. Write the name of the person who will be accountable for completing each step. This will often be you, but may also be members of your team or people you ask to help you.

Complete your action plan for your first goal in the space provided on the Action Plan Worksheet on page 16. You can also download a blank action plan template to use for your other goals at www.DailyActionLog.com.

Once you have a first-draft action plan for each of your goals, review them weekly. As you implement actions every day and make progress toward completing your goals, edit your action plans to improve their accuracy.

> **Note to Business Leaders**
>
> Many companies have their own format for documenting action plans. In fact, complex, elaborate projects are often best served using a sophisticated tracking tool like Microsoft Project. Whatever you use, make sure the steps, the person responsible for completing the steps, and the completion dates are clear.

First Week Goals

Throughout the Daily Action Log, you will have the opportunity to decide what your action steps are each day, and then summarize your week's progress. On that summary page, you will set your goals for the coming week. The question you will answer is, "Given where you are right now, what will you achieve this coming week?"

So, consider your ninety-day goals, where you are now (your starting point), and decide what you will achieve in your first week. Caution: this is not a to-do list exercise where you record all the things you want to complete today. This is only for those specific items that align with your ninety-day goals.

> **Your Action—First Week Goals**
>
> Use the First Week Goals worksheet on page 17 to write your goals for this week. There is space for five goals here and on each weekly summary page in the Daily Action Log. I suggest you focus on just five goals each week until you increase your goal-achieving capacity and capability.
> You can also download a blank copy of this worksheet at
> www.DailyActionLog.com.

Are you feeling critical about the size of your goals? It's okay to start small—just start! You can always set another goal once you've achieved the first one. Plus, achieving a small goal will help you to build momentum and give you a sense of accomplishment.

If you're like many goal-oriented people, you may have the tendency to set huge goals or take on quite a lot concurrently and risk not finishing them within ninety days. Following the Daily Action Log will help you learn the right balance for you.

Let's get started and learn from your experiences each day. You can always adjust your next ninety-day period.

* * *

Once you've completed your goals exercises, you're ready to learn about the three types of action in chapter 2.

Twelve-Month Goals

Write at least two goals in each category that you will achieve in the next twelve months.

Today's date: _____ Goal date: _____

By _____, I will...
    (goal date)

Financial

_____
_____
_____

Business/Career

_____
_____
_____

Health/Fitness

_____
_____
_____

Relationships

_____
_____
_____

Overall Happiness

_____
_____
_____

Download this template in convenient 8.5" x 11" size at
www.DailyActionLog.com

Ninety-Day Goals

Write your goals for the next ninety days with your twelve-month goals as a guide.

Today's date: _____ Goal date: _____

By _____, I will…
        (goal date)

Financial

_____
_____
_____

Business/Career

_____
_____
_____

Health/Fitness

_____
_____
_____

Relationships

_____
_____
_____

Overall Happiness

_____
_____
_____

Download this template in convenient 8.5" x 11" size at
www.DailyActionLog.com

Required Weekly Progress Rate

For each goal, follow the steps below:

1. Evaluate your starting point—where you are right now.

2. Identify the gap from where you are now to your ninety-day goal. (For example, today you weigh 190 pounds. Your goal is 178 pounds. Your gap is 190 - 178 = 12 pounds.)

3. Calculate your required weekly rate. Use twelve weeks (ninety days is 12.85 weeks).
   Required weekly rate = gap / 12 (weeks)

4. Use this rate to help you plan your weekly goals.

Goal	Goal	Starting Point	Gap	Weekly Rate = Gap / 12
e.g. Weigh 178 lbs.	178	190	12	1.0 per week
				per week
				per week
				per week
				per week
				per week
				per week
				per week
				per week
				per week

Download this template in convenient 8.5" x 11" size at
www.DailyActionLog.com

Action Plan Worksheet

1. Select one of your goals for this action plan and write it here. Your goal:

   _____

2. Complete this table with at least five steps you will take toward completing your goal.

Action Step	By Whom	By When	Notes
1.			
2.			
3.			
4.			
5.			
6.			
7.			
8.			
9.			
10.			

3. Review your action plan.

   a. Will all these steps get you to your goal, or are there more steps needed?

   b. Do you need to do them all yourself, or can other people help you?

   c. Are the dates reasonable?

4. What one action can you take to get started and build momentum in the next seventy-two hours? (This can be a subset of the above action steps.)

Note: a full page action plan like the one above is available on our website. There is also a more comprehensive version. Choose the one best suited to your needs.

Download this template in convenient 8.5" x 11" size at
www.DailyActionLog.com

First Week Goals

Refer to your Ninety-Day Goals worksheet to remind yourself what you strive to achieve in these next ninety days.

Now consider your required weekly progress rate from chapter 1 and other factors (your available capacity, help you have, prerequisite steps, etc.), and decide on the goals you will hit in your first week.

Today's date: _____   Goal date: _____

 By _____, **I will...**
    (goal date)

1. _____

2. _____

3. _____

4. _____

5. _____

Download this template in convenient 8.5" x 11" size at
www.DailyActionLog.com

CHAPTER 2

The Basics of Daily Action

To help you get in the right frame of mind to take action toward your goals each day, it might help to understand a few basic principles of daily action. Of course if you just can't wait to get started, go ahead and start, but come back soon and read this chapter.

This entire chapter aligns with what I call the Science of Success, the biology and quantum physics at work that enable you to successfully achieve our goals. Pay close attention throughout this chapter to better understand why daily action is so powerful.

In this chapter, I'll start by describing intention, as this is one important key to creating the results you want. Next, I'll share what I call the three types of action. While many of us only use one type of action, when we use all three working together we are incredibly powerful and achieve our goals faster than we would otherwise. I'll end the chapter with discussion about personal accountability. Ultimately in this process, you are accountable to yourself if you truly want to hit your goals.

Holding an Intention

Before we talk about actions, I want to help you appreciate the power of intention. If your intentions are clear, it becomes easier to identify the actions to take.

Let's start with some definitions to help us understand what we mean by intention.

Intend: to have in mind as something to be done or brought about.

Intention: the end or object intended; purpose.[2]

When you hold an intention, you are deliberate and clear in your mind about the results you want to create.

Often, we are not clear about what we want. Rather, we bounce through life following a path like a ball in a pinball machine—getting bounced and knocked all over the place. Having clarity about your purpose, your path, or how you want to experience your life is what intention is all about.

You can hold an intention for your day or for a portion of your day, like during a meeting or phone call. You can hold an intention for how you want to feel and what you want to experience. Intention is all about having clarity in your mind about what experience you want to create and then having trust and allowing your experience to align with your intention.

For example, I usually meditate in the morning and write down what my intention is for the day before I start. I frequently get intuitive ideas or inspirations during or after the meditation that support my intention—then it's up to me to act on them. If I did not hold the intention in the first place, I'm not sure I would receive those ideas. (I call these ideas and inspirations "intuitive hits.")

Note to Business Leaders

Intentions work for teams, too. In fact, when multiple people share the same intention, articulated the same way, the chance is greater that it will come true than if just the leader holds that intention. For example, let's say your team is helping you prepare a sales presentation to a prospective customer whose account could exceed $5 million this year. The whole team could hold the intention to convert this prospect into a $5 million customer.

Similarly, if you conduct team-based improvement projects, such as kaizen events, the whole team could reinforce their objective as an intention. For example, they might hold as their intention "to successfully implement our changes and achieve a 30 percent productivity improvement."

Last, if you are in network marketing, your entire team could hold the intention to recruit the perfect people to become distributors and join your team.

I have also been teaching my two boys that they create their experiences, and that they can hold an intention for what they want to create. For example, during the summer before entering fourth grade, my older son learned from other students that his assigned teacher had a reputation for yelling at the kids. You can imagine how nervous he was that he would have a horrible experience for the entire year!

During the first week of school, we worked on the intentions he set in an evening routine before bed to replace the fear of having an awful day with a mean teacher with more positive, empowering experiences. For example,

Dad: "What's your intention for tomorrow?"

Son: "I'm going to have a great day!"

Then, when he gets home from school,

Dad: "How was your day?"

Son: "Dad, it was the best day ever!"

Turns out, he loved his teacher and had a wonderful experience in fourth grade. We worked on helping him to create his experiences (and therefore his results) in other areas, too. Here were some of his other intentions that year:

- "I'm going to pay attention to the teacher's instructions."

- "I will make at least one new friend today."

- "I will have fun today."

- "I'm going to be a great listener."

I love hearing both my sons' reports at the end of the day. We talk about how they created the results they wanted and how their intentions came true. Or, if the results were not what they intended, we often identify some action or outcome that didn't align with their intention. This serves as a tool of self-awareness for the next time they're in a similar situation.

It helps if you believe that your intention will come true. If you are unsure, you're introducing doubt into the process of creating results.

Intentions work best when you are certain they will come true and you expect them to happen.

In *The Biology of Belief*, Dr. Bruce Lipton describes how our biological makeup, right down to the cellular level, is impacted by our experiences and beliefs. Dr. Lipton explains that our subconscious mind is much more powerful than our conscious mind and the majority of our subconscious "programming" occurs during early childhood. When our subconscious mind receives a stimulus, it responds based on the cellular programming developed early in our lives. The good news is, we can change this programming.

By studying our response and deciding to change it, we can. Our behavior and ability is not solely based on our genes; we can influence it with the power of our intentions. What you believe will dictate your results, so choose beliefs that support you.

Additionally, intentions work best when you're in a constant state of gratitude—you appreciate all that you have and you openly and genuinely share your gratitude.

Your Action—Intention for Today

Each day, begin by stating a clear intention for what you want to experience. It might be a state, such as, "Today I will experience _____" (fun, happiness, calm, focus, or any other quality you desire). Or your intention can be an outcome, such as "Today I will _____" (have a great meeting with a client, be super-productive and clear my desk by five o'clock, or close two sales). You might choose to be specific with numbers, such as "Today I will _____" (write ten pages, confirm $50k of revenue, or meet two new people).

The fun part about intentions is that you get to choose what you want to experience. Once you're clear in your mind about what you want, trust that the Science of Success will work to support you. (See www.DailyActionLog.com for more information about the Science of Success.)

Three Types of Action

I teach my clients that there are three types of action: daily habits, planned actions, and inspired actions. This Daily Action Log incorporates all three types because when you learn to use all three you get results faster. Let me briefly describe each for you.

- Daily habits—proven success habits we follow on a daily basis. These are things like visualizing goals, saying affirmations, meditating, reading, exercising, and other disciplines proven to accelerate our goal achievement. We trust that these daily disciplines will help us achieve our goals by enabling us to manage stress and stay focused, by allowing us to keep our energy and motivation levels up, and by triggering the biology and physics of goal achievement. This helps us to recognize ideas and resources that are there to accelerate our results and goal achievement and to take action on our ideas.

- Planned actions—the actions we take as a result of writing an action plan for a specific result or goal. Following the steps that we say we will take moves us toward the results we want. For example, if you want to complete a marathon six months from now, you might create a schedule of distances you plan to run each week and each day. That run would be a planned action. Or, if we want to start a new business venture, we clearly define the steps we plan to take over the next ninety days (or longer) in a business plan.

- Inspired actions—these are actions we take in response to an intuitive hit, inspiration, or idea. We may find solutions to a problem we currently face or receive a delightful string of creative ideas. These solutions and ideas will pop into our awareness, seemingly out of nowhere (because we are disciplined in following the daily habits)—it is now up to us to take the actions inspired by our ideas. Note that initially you will not likely find these actions on your action plan. Rather, these will be special instructions that you receive in the moment—instructions from some higher place of knowing. This is powerful stuff, so don't ignore the signals you get; act on them as quickly as you are able!

All three types of action will get you closer to your goals—the important thing is that you take action and move forward rather than sit back and over think your next move. Remember, as Jack Canfield shares in his books, workshops, and audio programs, "the universe rewards action." By taking action we are in motion toward our destination, making things happen along the way. If we stay still, nothing happens. So, go get your rewards by taking action now!

2011 candidate for President of Ireland, Sean Gallagher—named one of Ireland's top entrepreneurs in 2006—shared a quote with me that illustrates this point well, "A man who waits for everything to be perfect before taking the next step will spend his entire life standing on one leg."

Even if you get started down a path and soon realize that a different course of action would be more effective, trust that you were supposed to gain some knowledge or learn some lesson from following that initial path. Ask yourself, "What did I learn?" and then incorporate those lessons as you move forward.

This Daily Action Log incorporates all three types of action and provides space for you to record the lessons you learn along the way.

Daily Habits

You've probably heard a million times about all these things that are good for you, especially if you do them every day. Well, maybe not a million but enough for you to be aware of what many of them are. After all, I'm guessing you brush your teeth at least once a day—it's now a daily habit. Not that brushing your teeth with help you achieve your most important goals, but it does prove that you can get results (clean teeth) by practicing daily habits.

The good news is that there are many daily habits that are proven to accelerate your goal achievement. You'll find that those I've selected for this Daily Action Log are some of the most powerful, impactful habits you can employ. Here is a list of the ones included in the Daily Action Log, followed by a short description of each.

- Visualizing your goals as already achieved

- Saying affirmations for your goals

- Expressing appreciation and gratitude

- Meditating

- Journaling

- Reading

- Exercising

- "Letting Go"

- Optional Habit

> **Note to Business Leaders**
>
> Napoleon Hill, author of *Think and Grow Rich*, interviewed some of the greatest business leaders of the industrial revolution while researching his book. These included Andrew Carnegie, Henry Ford, Harvey Firestone, George Eastman, and Charles M. Schwab, to name a few. When you read *Think and Grow Rich,* you'll recognize similarities to the list of daily habits I reference in *Act Now!*
>
> These and similar daily habits helped these business leaders build great companies. Can you recognize that getting your team to follow them can drive great results for your company, too?

Visualizing Your Goals as Already Achieved

Visualization is creating an active picture in your mind. Think of it as a movie with you as the lead actor, and see the scene from your own eyes. Design your "mind movie" to see and feel your life as you would experience it if your goals were already achieved. The most impactful visualizations will include a clear vision of your life after your goal is achieved and will trigger genuine feelings that fit your scene.

According to Napoleon Hill, author of the classic personal-success book *Think and Grow Rich*, Andrew Carnegie himself regularly practiced visualization and became the richest man in the world. In fact, the five hundred men that Hill studied for his book all practiced visualizing their goals as achieved and attributed this as a key reason they rose to great wealth. Indeed, this is an important practice to accelerate progress toward any goal you have set.

When you first define a new goal, take a few minutes to sit quietly and design in your mind the scene of that goal achieved. What do you see? How do you know the goal is complete?

For example, if your goal is to finish a marathon, see yourself crossing the finish line. If it's to weigh a certain amount, see yourself standing on the scale reading that exact number. Maybe your goal is to confirm a $1 million contract, so see yourself signing the contract and shaking your customer's hand. If it is to improve your department's productivity by 30 percent, you can visualize the productivity reports with results that exceed your goal and see your team steadily working without problems to distract them.

It is also critical to amp up the feelings associated with your successful accomplishment. Let yourself be in the moment and feel the excitement, joy, pride, relief, or whatever feeling fits your scene.

Once you've created this visualization, replay it every day.

Your Action—Visualize Your Goals

I recommend visualizing your most important goals twice per day, in the morning when you wake up and just before you go to sleep at night.

When you first wake, your brain is still experiencing alpha waves before becoming fully alert. Visualizing at this time will help because the alpha state enables creativity and learning at a faster and deeper level. Also, what you experience during your last thirty minutes before bed plays in your unconscious mind during the night.

When you wake in the morning, sit comfortably and close your eyes. Recall the image of your life with your goal complete, and feel all the great feelings associated with your success. Notice: Where are you? Who is with you? What do you hear? Describe what you see and use vivid colors. Now that you've achieved your goal, describe and experience the emotions. Enjoy that moment and tighten your fist to anchor that feeling of success. Allow yourself to smile. This should take less than a minute.

Just before bed, repeat the same exercise.

You'll soon find that this vision is so real to you that its coming true is a foregone conclusion!

Bonus action: Create a vision board by collecting images that represent your visualization. You can put them on an actual board, or keep them as digital images on your computer or mobile device.

Saying Affirmations for Your Goals

Affirmations are positive, present-tense statements that reinforce the vision of your goal as already complete. In Principle 10 of *The Success Principles*, Jack Canfield describes nine guidelines for creating effective affirmations. They are as follows:

1. Start with the words "I am."

2. State it in the positive.

3. Use the present tense.

4. Keep it brief.

5. Make it specific.

6. Include an action verb ending in "-ing."

7. Include at least one dynamic emotion or feeling word.

8. Make affirmations for yourself, not for others.

9. Add the words, "Or something better."

The affirmations that helped me complete my first marathon in January 2000 included, "I am excitedly crossing the finish line of the Disney Marathon, ready to do it again" and "My muscles are strong; I am powerful; I have endurance; I have speed."

(I love Lightning McQueen in the animated Disney movie *Cars* when he's preparing for the big race saying his affirmation, "Speed…I am speed!" His version is better than mine because he uses the words "I am.")

I used similar affirmations to help me complete my first triathlon in 2010, but this time using the word "energetically" rather than "excitedly" because I wanted to experience the race and then have energy to enjoy the rest of the day at the beach with my family.

Tie the affirmation you write to your visualization for that goal. Using the above examples, you might say, "I am happily standing on the scale, reading my perfect body weight of 173 pounds." Or, "I am enthusiastically shaking hands with my customer and confirming the $1 million contract." Or, "I am excitedly congratulating my team for hitting the 30 percent productivity targets."

Experience the visualization, remembering to engage your feelings and all five senses. Then, say your affirmations out loud. Your spoken words will anchor your visualization deeper into your unconscious mind.

Your Reticular Activating System

Your reticular activating system (RAS) is the part of your brain that acts as a filter. This filter is important because we receive two billion bits of information per second, and it would be impossible to manage every one of them. Your RAS is the gatekeeper that only lets through to your conscious awareness the inputs it believes are important. With visualization and affirmations, you begin to redefine what is important by repetition and the intensity of emotion associated with your goals. Soon, you begin to notice resources and opportunities because your RAS has begun to let them through to your conscious mind. Now, you just need to take action on them!

As with your visualization, repeat your affirmation at least twice each day, just after waking up, and then again just before you go to bed so that your unconscious mind works on your goals while you're asleep.

Your Action—Affirmations

Use the guidelines above to write at least one affirmation for each goal. Visualize each goal as achieved, and while you're still focused on that, write a statement that follows the guidelines and describes how you're feeling and what you're doing (remember, use an "-ing" verb). Take your time, have fun, and edit your affirmation until it resonates with you. Use the Affirmations worksheet on page 54.

Once you are satisfied, copy your affirmation onto a 3" x 5" card or type it into your mobile device and review it often.

Say your affirmations twice each day, immediately after you complete your visualizations. You should be able to say them all in just a few minutes.

Bonus action: Record your affirmations and listen to them on your computer, iPod, smart phone, or other device.

Expressing Appreciation and Gratitude

Appreciation and gratitude are important feelings that have wonderful benefits for our health and ability to attract the results we want.

Appreciation is the act of being openly thankful and recognizing our own contributions or the contributions of others. Appreciate yourself for your job well done, your efforts to stay on track, having kept your commitments, etc. All this builds trust and confidence in yourself so that you will excitedly venture forward to take on whatever is necessary to succeed at the next level. Your positive self-talk of appreciation makes the game of achieving your goals fun for you to keep playing.

Similarly, appreciating others for their contributions toward helping you create the results you want keeps them feeling good about their efforts. They will want to continue working or playing with you because of your genuine, thoughtful, and caring attitude.

Gratitude is a feeling that goes beyond satisfaction—you are happy about what you have and do not take anything for granted. A feeling of thanksgiving fills your heart as you recognize the roles of everyone around you in supporting your success. You express this internal feeling of gratitude through external appreciation.

Coherence and The Field

With appreciation and gratitude, you more easily reach the biological state of "coherence," where your heart rate, breathing, and brain-wave activity reach an optimum state. The Institute of HeartMath has done numerous studies and found that appreciation and gratitude are central to enabling the desirable state of coherence.[3] In this biological state, our stress levels are reduced and our productivity and effectiveness are increased.

Beyond biology, appreciation and gratitude also help us from a quantum physics perspective. In the book, *The Field*, Lynn McTaggert shares extensive research into what quantum physicists call the Zero Point Field, the Quantum Field, or simply The Field. At a quantum level this field of energy is present among all things in the universe, like a giant ocean within which we all exist. (In Disney's movie, The Incredibles, the character Syndrome brags about learning to harness "zero point technology" as the secret to his superpowers). Our thoughts and desires ripple the Zero Point Field,[4] and we seem to attract ideas and resources that align with our most dominant thoughts and desires.

Appreciation and gratitude help us enter a state of allowing, which makes it easier for us to recognize the ideas and resources that are subsequently attracted to us.

In an opposite state, where perhaps we are angry at ourselves for making a mistake, we are more likely to resist any help or support that may appear—in fact, it's likely we won't even see it.

Appreciation and gratitude together create the state of allowing that helps us recognize a helpful resource, then feel an even deeper sense of gratitude, which then attracts even more ideas or resources. It creates a virtuous cycle that accelerates our success while making others around us feel great about their ongoing role. It's truly a win–win!!

To help develop this as a habit, look for reasons to feel grateful every day. Look in the mirror and appreciate yourself and emphasize the positive rather than criticize yourself. I don't care how corny you might think this is—do it today, and notice how amazing you feel.

Your Action—Appreciation and Gratitude

Each day, ask yourself, "What am I grateful for right now?" If you're grateful for a person, express your appreciation to that person in some way—vocalize it, write a card, or send an e-mail or text message. If you're grateful for things you have, simply experience that satisfaction. Make sure you express appreciation to at least one other person each day.

Each night when you get ready for bed, look in the mirror and tell yourself how much you appreciate your efforts, your progress, and your results.

Meditating

Meditation is the practice of emptying your mind of all conscious thought. There are many forms of meditation and guided visualization. You can listen to a leader's voice and allow your unconscious mind freedom to respond while your conscious mind is quiet. You can sit quietly and allow your thoughts to drift away while you enjoy a quiet and peaceful state. Or, these practices can be fun and interactive; you can go on a visual journey to discover the deeper meaning of your purpose in life or to receive answers from your unconscious mind to help you solve many of life's questions.[5]

However you choose to meditate, know that it will provide you with a number of proven benefits. Studies show that regular meditation practice reduces stress and sharpens intuition.[6]

Note to Business Leaders: Meditation in Business

Beyond the many examples of entrepreneurs who meditate to spark their intuitive ideas, some business leaders of large corporations recognize the power of meditation, too. Larry Ellison, Oracle CEO, asks his executives to meditate three times each afternoon.[7] Other meditation devotees include Mike Milken, Bill George, Renetta McCann, Phil Jackson, Larry Brilliant, and Bob Shapiro.[8] Robert Stiller's Green Mountain Coffee Roasters, Inc., even has a dedicated meditation room where meditation is taught regularly.[9]

By setting aside the preconceived notion of a meditator as a bald man in a robe sitting in the lotus position, the corporate world can benefit greatly from a sound meditation practice. Imagine holding a meeting with your staff where everyone easily manages the demands of your high-paced business. They are able to set aside all the clutter of their lives and focus on the issues at hand with great clarity. Now *that* is a tremendous foundation for a high-performing team!

I strive to meditate daily and know that I manage to keep more calm and centered during stressful times, get great ideas out of the blue, and feel more present as a result. My friend Dr. Deb Sandella told me of a story in which the Dalai Lama said, "I have so much to do today I had better meditate for two hours rather than one." I appreciate why he says this and make every effort to meditate during my most stressful, busy days.

I strongly believe in helping you improve your health and intuitive powers, and encourage you to practice some form of meditation regularly. The easiest way to start a meditation practice is to listen to an audio guide, or simply close your eyes and notice your breathing for a few minutes as you inhale and exhale. Meditation is something you can do in just five minutes or for well over an hour.

The first time I met spiritual teacher Deirdre Hade, she led the whole meeting room of about one hundred people in a guided meditation that was profound for me. Time stood still while I journeyed and engaged my unconscious mind. I had incredibly deep insights that I quickly wrote down when we finished. It was exciting! I later learned that we had meditated for an hour and forty-five minutes! Meditation can provide a similar experience for you, too, as you develop this daily habit.

If you're looking for some recorded meditations to get you started, visit www.DailyActionLog.com.

Your Action—Meditation

If you've never meditated before, you may choose to buy some recorded meditations to listen to. There are hundreds of them out there so experiment and find ones that work best for you.

Schedule time in your day to meditate, and keep that schedule.

If you have a recorded meditation, simply turn it on and listen while you sit quietly. If not, sit quietly, focus on your breath, and observe your inhalations and exhalations. If you have any chatter from your conscious mind, simply say "thank you" and let it go for now. Sit as long as you'd like.

That's it! Easy, isn't it?

Journaling

Journaling is the practice of letting your mind flow and capturing your thoughts on paper. Like meditation, there are many methods of journaling. Julie Cameron, author of *The Artist's Way*, suggests spending a few minutes writing just after you wake. This helps you purge the thoughts and distractions you have from the night's dreams, enabling you to start your day with a clear head.

I like to journal right after meditating, as my mind is clear and alert at that time. I capture amazing insights and ideas right after meditating. Writing also helps ground the positive energy I experience from meditating.

You can also journal when you're stuck. Simply grab some paper and write whatever comes to you. You can often create a breakthrough and get unstuck in just a few minutes as solutions magically present themselves.

Sometimes your mind is racing and you just can't focus, which is especially problematic at bedtime. This is another great time to journal. Begin writing to get what's in your head down on paper. When you do this, you're acknowledging the thoughts, often clarifying them by working out your ideas, and you can then move on without the mind chatter. Plus, you're less worried about forgetting because you can reference your written notes later.

With today's technology, you can experiment with typing yourself a note or sending yourself an e-mail. You can use a voice recorder, leave yourself a voice mail, or some other alternative to writing in a paper journal. There are apps for your mobile device you can try. You decide what works best for you.

Get a notebook, write today's date on the top of a page, and begin writing anything that comes to mind. Journaling is as simple as that.

If you want a more structured assignment, try one of the following:

- *Journal first thing in the morning, as soon as you're awake, to capture anything that may still be present in your unconscious mind while you can still access it.* Write about your dreams or anything else you can remember from the night before. See if you can write until you fill two or three pages.

- *Journal immediately after meditating.* You may find that the most amazing ideas and insights are present for you at this time. Or, perhaps there are no breakthrough ideas today—if so, capture whatever comes to mind. These thoughts often have value and will make sense later.

- *Think of what you're grateful for, and write about it.* If you appreciate yourself while you do, it will count as both journaling and expressing appreciation in your Daily Action Log.

- *Visualize your goals as achieved and describe it in writing.* Emphasize how you feel now that your goals are complete. This will count as journaling and visualizing in your Daily Action Log.

- *Just before bed, recognize all the thoughts that are flying around and write them in your journal.* This will clear your mind and allow you to enjoy a peaceful sleep.

You can journal for just a few minutes or much longer if you have the time and your internal engine is providing a steady stream of insights and solutions. Play with the different methods and see what resonates with you.

Reading (or Similar Media)

Reading includes books, e-books, magazines, blog posts, newsletters, and any other media that engages your mind. You can read to learn more about topics that interest you or help you develop your expertise, or you may read purely for pleasure. In all cases, you expand your mind and engage your imagination, which in turn helps to keep you fresh and youthful. Here is a tip from Brad Isaac I found to be true: "Once you make reading a habit, you'll enjoy reading the books in your chosen career as well."[10]

Audio books and audio learning programs also count in this category, as they also expand your mind and imagination. CDs and MP3s are convenient and portable and provide the opportunity to learn from an expert interview or other educational program. It's also a great way to multitask and inject new knowledge into your brain—you can't read while driving, but you can listen to an audio book and learn that way.

Whether a book that you underline, highlight, and write in or an MP3 where you listen to someone's words, over time this practice can give you more knowledge and fill your brain with fresh ideas. The knowledge and fresh ideas can then be applied as you break through barriers you encounter or fuel creativity as you strive to achieve your goals more quickly.

Your Action—Reading

If you read just thirty minutes a day, in about one hundred days you will have completed an amount comparable to a college course! Your action therefore is to schedule some reading time into your daily calendar.

Grab a book, open it, and read for a few minutes. If you can only afford to read for five minutes, that's better than not having bothered. You might find that you're really into what you're reading and decide to skip the television tonight.

Exercising

Exercising is the act of getting your body moving. It includes aerobic exercise, such as running, biking, or Zumba class, which increases your heart rate. Exercising also includes anaerobic exercise, such as resistance training like weight lifting. Exercise raises your endurance and energy levels; strengthens your heart, lungs, and other organs; and manages your stress levels and weight.

All forms of exercise are helpful, but some forms are better than others depending on your goals. For example, if you are interested in losing weight, expert nutritionist JJ Virgin tell us that weight lifting and burst training are the way to go (check out the Resources page on www.DailyActionLog. com). To complete a triathlon, you need to practice swimming, biking, and running, as well as weight lifting or other cross-training. If you have a ski trip planned, you might want to build your leg muscles and do some aerobic training to build your endurance. You get the idea.

Frank Booth, a physiologist at the University of Missouri, Columbia, and executive director of Researchers Against Inactivity-Related Disorders, has studied direct and indirect costs of physical inactivity. For example, in the United States the costs associated with a sedentary lifestyle were more than $150 billion during 1987 (expressed in 2000 dollars). Yikes!

Even if you don't have a current fitness goal, exercise will help you reduce stress, clear your head, and become more productive. And, it becomes easier if you do it every day!

So, what if you don't have any fitness goals? Do you still need to exercise? Yes!

Your energy level and health are important for all your goals. If you're always tired or sick it will be hard to take any action toward your goals. Think of how great you'll feel when you achieve them. Be proactive, exercise a few times per week, and take care of your body.

> **Your Action—Exercising**
>
> Check with your doctor to see if you have any restrictions, and find a form of exercise that is within your capability.
>
> Commit to doing some form of exercise at least three times each week. Schedule it on your calendar.
>
> Bonus action: Choose a friend to be an exercise buddy and hold each other accountable for your workouts.

"Letting Go"

"Letting Go", or releasing, is the act of simply dropping our problems, concerns, issues, limiting beliefs, etc. While this is simple to do, it's not necessarily easy. We've learned to hold on tightly to them—we love the story of our woe and strife. Wouldn't life be easier if we didn't have problems, concerns, issues, and limiting beliefs?

We tend to magnify our problems, concerns, and issues by allowing the negative emotion and energy we associate with an event to creep in and distract us. Interestingly, we are the ones who assign meaning to events that we experience (read the box "Our Unconscious Mind" for more about how we assign meaning to events). To make matters worse, we amplify the negative emotional charge associated with each event we define as negative and allow ourselves to get twisted up as a result. I love this quote by Mark Twain: "I've had thousands of problems in my life, most of which never actually happened."

Researchers in neuroscience, psychology, and other biological sciences have studied how we react to situations and events in our lives. An event we experience has no inherent meaning—our unconscious mind creates a meaning because it wants to make sense of things. Other functions of our unconscious mind include keeping us safe and finding evidence that its interpretations of the world are right ("See, I told you you're not good enough…").

Our Unconscious Mind

Our unconscious mind means well, but…

According to Sean Smith, the coach from whom I learned neuro-linguistic programming (NLP), our unconscious mind can be characterized by the following three statements:

1. It protects us and keeps us safe.

2. It wants to make sense of things.

3. It likes to be right.

When we experience an event, our unconscious mind assigns it a meaning. The meaning is one it believes will protect us in the future. It files the event and associated meaning in a way that makes sense given all our other past experiences. And because it likes to be right, it will collect evidence from other experiences and future events to prove the past meanings it assigned to events are right. Thus, our beliefs are born.

Ideas like "I'm not worthy of success," "It's risky to accept challenges," or "My needs are not as important as other people's needs" may have their roots in an event you experienced as a two-year-old while on a play date. Your unconscious mind has led you to learn patterns that characterize who you've become and how you think.

Many of us could use some rewiring!

Over time, the play among these functions of our unconscious mind creates our beliefs, which can manifest as huge issues and barriers that hold us back. These issues and barriers, as deeply rooted as they may be, are only as real and powerful as we've made them.

Sure, you might still have a large debt, an unfulfilling relationship, or challenges at work. But as long as you have stress around these issues it will be more difficult to handle them. Remember, what you resist persists. By letting go of your emotional attachments, you are able to move more easily through your issues.

Accepting that our problems, concerns, issues, and beliefs are just made up can help us release them, and in the process set ourselves free from the emotional baggage we've assigned to them. Once we've done this, we are free to move forward toward our goals, completely open and unencumbered.

At this point, you might be thinking, "Wait a minute—you're saying I made up these problems?" Well, yes—I am. Bear with me on this. If you can develop the habit of letting go, you'll clear an enormous amount of emotional space to be used for your goal achievement and to create the life you want.

I've been trained in many methods and techniques of helping people to identify where they have issues and barriers that hold them back, to shift their perspective, and to ultimately free themselves. Deeply held beliefs that limit us require rewiring or reframing the meaning we've assigned to them. This can be done over a series of coaching sessions using a variety of the methods I share here. Often, though, by choosing to release the emotional charge associated with these problems, concerns, issues, and beliefs, you can begin to make great progress by self-administering these methods.

Methods of letting go are simple to learn and incorporate into your daily habits. The only limit to their effectiveness is your belief. If you don't believe the methods will work, they probably won't work for you, yet they may work well for someone else. If you find you're stuck, you can have a skilled coach help you.

Here is a quick primer to get you started. Look at the Resources page on www.DailyActionLog.com for more information about these methods.

Some of these techniques you already know something about; in this case we're applying them to help you learn to let go. I've used each of these techniques to help other people break through their issues, and I use them myself when I find issues beginning to get in my way.

Journaling—You can dump your thoughts onto paper and affirm "While I write about this problem/concern/issue/belief, I know it dissolves and I am free." Write whatever comes to mind and just notice what you write without judgment. If you choose, you can then tear up or even burn that paper, or put a giant check mark on it, signifying the issue is now closed.

Total Truth Letter—In *The Success Principles*, Jack Canfield describes the Total Truth Letter. Basically, you can write a letter to the person (or other source of your problem), express the anger and hurt you feel, and express in words forgiveness and love. When you're finished, know the issue has been released and is no longer a burden for you. You don't even need to send the letter, and you may decide to tear it up or burn it.

The Sedona Method—Hale Dwoskin, CEO and Director of Training at Sedona Training Associates, teaches The Sedona Method, which he learned from his mentor, Lester Levinson. After being given only a few months to live, Lester developed and practiced this method of Letting Go and lived another twenty years.[11] There are a number of ways to practice The Sedona Method; each is an effective way to dissolve the issues with simple repetition. The most basic way to practice The Sedona Method is by asking yourself the following:

- *Could* I let this go?

- *Would* I let this go?

- *When?*

Allow yourself to let go, even if just for a moment. Go through these questions as often as you like.

Ho'oponopono—I learned the form called "Self I-Dentity Ho'oponopono" from Dr. Ihaleakala Hew Len and Joe Vitale, as described in the book *Zero Limits: The Secret Hawaiian System for Wealth, Health, Peace, and More.* Ho'oponopono is a Hawaiian word that means 'to make right' or 'to rectify an error.' Therapists often facilitate a disagreement between two people using this method with four simple statements: "I love you. I'm sorry. Please forgive me. Thank you." In Dr. Hew Len's Self I-Dentity Ho'oponopono, you have dialogue with the Divine (whatever that means to you) with the same four statements. Repeating these phrases can dissolve your issues. You can read about Dr. Hew Len's fascinating story and the results this method can deliver in *Zero Limits*.

Meditation—You may find that stating your issue and simply holding the intention to dissolve your issue while meditating for fifteen to thirty minutes will resolve it, or at least give you insights about how to dissolve the issue.

Emotional Freedom Technique (EFT)—EFT is a simple method created by Gary Craig by which you follow a routine of "tapping" on a number of points on your body. Like acupuncture, the tapping disrupts your body's energy meridians. Following the EFT tapping protocol will help you disassociate any emotion from past memories and dissolve your issue.

Neuro-linguistic programming (NLP)—NLP is a set of techniques which were first developed in the 1970s by Richard Bandler and John Grinder after studying the behaviors and beliefs of individuals deemed super successful. From more than three decades of study and application of various methods to help people become "unstuck," NLP techniques can literally rewire your unconscious mind. NLP can help you break free from your issues and excel toward the success you want, even if you're not sure what your root issues are. You may require a coach certified in NLP to help you apply this method of Letting Go.

RIM—"Releasing your Inner Magician" (RIM) is a facilitated exercise developed by Dr. Deb Sandella. The facilitator will guide the client in a closed-eyes exercise that "walks on the rim" between the conscious and unconscious mind. The facilitator's questions help you to disassociate the perceived issue from any emotional charge, thus neutralizing the issue. As with NLP, you may require a coach experienced in RIM to help you dissolve issues and eliminate barriers.

Begin with whichever of these methods of Letting Go seems to resonate with you. Try it and see what happens. You can expect to minimize the negative impact of any emotional energy attached to your perceived issues, which will enable you to carry on as if the issue was not ever a barrier for you. Sometimes past issues are totally resolved in just a few minutes, while some issues require consistent attention or even facilitated help from a coach. If you find that you're stuck and unable to break free from your issues, refer to www.DailyActionLog.com.

Your Action—Letting Go

At first it may seem unnecessary to practice a form of letting go every day, but I know people who spend a few minutes every morning using the Sedona Method to release. I know people who do the same with ho'oponopono. Of course, there are people who journal and meditate each day. And NLP or RIM sessions can be incorporated into coaching sessions.

I invite you to notice when you're getting all twisted up because of some issue or problem. The first step is to recognize that you sometimes do this. Then make the conscious choice to let go of your emotional charge. You can use any of the methods described above, and over time you may find that you have a favorite that works best for you.

When you're ready, you can build this into a daily habit. Like many of the other habits, you may find that scheduling a time helps—you will need just a few minutes each day. To make it easy, I suggest sticking with one technique for a week or two until you are comfortable with it, and then move to another one. Over time, you'll know what makes the most sense for different situations.

Have fun with this one—it is meant to be easy and freeing!

Planned Actions

Before you decide the planned actions you will take on a daily basis, it helps if you first create an action plan for every goal you set. This gives you a starting point for your planned actions, which you can then adjust as you work on your action plan each week. With your action plan in hand, you can set specific goals for the week. These goals will align with your longer-term goals, but will also fit where you actually are today. Once you have clarity about what you want to accomplish this week, you will use the Rule of 5 each day to ensure you're making progress.

Let's talk about action plans, goals for the week, and the Rule of 5 in more detail.

Action Plans, Revisited

In chapter 1, you had an exercise to create action plans for each of your goals. Remind yourself of the steps you intend to follow by reviewing your actions plans weekly as they will help you decide your goals for each week.

If you have not completed the action plan worksheet on page 16, go ahead and invest time now.

Set Goals for the Week

Your action plan should give you a clear idea of what you plan to accomplish each week, especially if you monitor and edit it as you make progress.

Given your progress so far, the input from your action plan, and any other information that you need to factor in (such as your travel schedule, the availability of people you need to meet, etc.), you decide what it is you want to accomplish this week and define that as a goal.

Using some of our earlier examples, let's say your ninety-day goal is to complete a marathon. Your training schedule (action plan) says you should complete a sixteen-mile run this weekend, and you're a week behind in the actual distance of your long run, so you might decide to set a goal to run fifteen miles on Saturday.

Or, if your goal is to book a $1 million contract and you don't have any meetings scheduled for the week after next, this week you might decide to set a goal to make fifteen follow-up calls to schedule five appointments for your sales presentation.

The goals for the week should be manageable. These weekly goals will help you stay on track, manage your plan, and ultimately hit your goals on time or early.

> **Your Action—Weekly Goals**
>
> There is a section on the Weekly Summary log sheet for you to write your weekly goals. I encourage you to do this every week.
>
> Prior to setting your weekly goals, assess where you are. What progress have you made so far? Are you ahead of or behind schedule? Where are you compared to what your action plan suggests? What events do you know are coming this week?
>
> Now set your goals for the week. Write them in the Next Week's Goals box on your Weekly Summary log sheet.

The Rule of 5

Perhaps you've heard the question "How do you eat an elephant?" and the answer, "One bite at a time!"

To make progress toward even your largest goals requires you to take a little action every day. That is the basis of the principle called the Rule of 5—to take one bite at a time and five bites a day.

The Rule of 5 comes from advice that Jack Canfield and Mark Victor Hansen received from Ron Scolastico about their enormous goal of getting *Chicken Soup for the Soul* on the *New York Times* best-seller list. His advice included the analogy of chopping down the largest tree in the forest. If you were to take five swings with an axe into that tree every day, eventually it would come down. From this simple concept was born the Rule of 5.[12]

Simply, the Rule of 5 is do five things every day toward your most important goal(s).

Recognize that it's still important to have a plan, with milestones or targets to hit. As you decide what you're going to work on this week, you will consider your action plan, yet have flexibility as you anticipate inspired actions along the way.

Each day, simply decide the five actions (at minimum) that you will take toward your most important goals, and do these early in the day before you get distracted. Commit to completing these actions before you consider yourself finished for the day.

> **Your Action—Rule of 5**
>
> Each day, decide what five planned actions you will take, and write them on your Daily Action Log. Take into account your progress so far, your overall action plans, and your goals for the week.
>
> You will have more success if you do these five daily planned actions before you get involved in other less strategic actions that may eat up your available time and leave you with insufficient time to complete your planned actions.
>
> Bonus action: Decide the evening before what you will work on the next day so you can get a jump on your list first thing in the morning.

Inspired Actions

Inspired actions are just that—actions that you decide to take as a result of some inspiration. This inspiration is often what I call an intuitive hit. It's an "ah-ha" moment, an insight you get seemingly out of the blue. It might be something you dream at night and briefly remember in the morning, or it might be the proverbial light bulb that goes on in the middle of the day.

We all get intuitive hits. The question for you to consider is, what do you do when you get one? Are you momentarily excited, only to soon be distracted and forget what your idea was? Do you write it off as unrealistic, or not right for you? ("Oh, I couldn't do that!") Or, do you write it down and figure out how to put it into action?

Not every intuitive hit is a million-dollar idea. Although, I'm pretty sure you've had at least one million-dollar idea, even if you didn't pursue it. The first thing to recognize with these intuitive hits is that they come every day, many of them small course adjustments for our daily activity. They can be things like, "Call Chris this afternoon," "Attend the meeting at the library tonight," or "Take the Main Street exit rather than South Street."

While they do come every day, we're not always listening. We're often too distracted with our busy lives. Our brains are flying at supersonic speed, thinking about multiple things at once. It is nearly impossible to recognize these valuable nuggets at these times (which implies that we ought to consider ways to multitask less and create focus time). Can we slow down and quiet that overactive brain of ours so that it recognizes the intuitive hit in the first place?

This is exactly what some of the daily habits do for us. Meditation allows our overactive conscious mind to quiet down. Visualizing and affirming our goals fires up our reticular activating system (RAS) so it is on the lookout for things that match our goal as already achieved. It then points out their presence so we can take action on them. Exercising helps us manage stress and stay focused. Reading injects new knowledge and keeps our brain actively engaged, which thereby sharpens our critical-thinking skills. Letting go of issues and problems frees our mind from these distractions.

All these daily habits create an environment that is ripe for your intuition to flourish. It is because we are actively engaged in these daily habits that we begin to recognize more intuitive hits on a regular basis. The more we recognize, the more we can act on and benefit from them. This is a great goal accelerator!

What should you do when you recognize an intuitive hit? Capture it and act on it as quickly as is feasible. We don't always have a lot of time to react—if you're driving on the highway when your intuition says "Take the Main Street exit," and the Main Street exit is just a mile away, you have to decide right now to follow that intuitive hit.

You may have a strong sense that the answer to a critical question is "yes"—despite your initial impression that "no" is the right answer. Entertain the likelihood with all seriousness that "yes" is indeed the answer. If you need a day to check into things further then go ahead, and then decide "yes"!

It's a skill to learn to hear and then trust your intuition. Like learning any skill, you'll need to practice. Have faith and follow exactly what these intuitive hits suggest and see what happens. What do you have to lose? Usually the risk is so low that you may as well follow your intuitive hit. As you create a history of successes where following your intuition moved you toward your goals faster, you will trust them more and you will be more alert to their presence.

That's when things really get fun! You will likely find the size of the ideas you receive grows steadily, which allows your impact and results to also grow proportionately.

> There are many stories of people receiving some intuitive insight, acting upon it, and achieving a great result. In *Rolling Stone, The Beatles' 100 Greatest Songs*, Paul McCartney recounts how one night he awoke with music running through his head that was unlike any of the other songs he had written. "It fell out of bed," he once said about the origins of "Yesterday." "I had a piano by my bedside, and I must have dreamed it, because I tumbled out of bed and put my hands on the piano keys and I had a tune in my head. It was just all there, a complete thing. I couldn't believe it. It came too easily."[13]
>
> Chemist Friedrich August Kekulé was struggling to come up with the structure of benzene when he dreamed of a snake made of atoms taking its tail in its mouth. Benzene's structure is, in fact, a closed ring.[14]
>
> It would have been easy for McCartney and Kekulé to discard these ideas, as they were unexpected and totally different from their usual thinking. The world is glad they followed through and took inspired action! What other examples have you heard of? Do you have a history of your own inspired actions leading to great results?

> ### Your Action—Intuitive Hits
>
> First, be open to the possibility that you are constantly receiving ideas and intuitive hits, every day. As you continue to follow the daily habits, know you will recognize them more easily.
>
> Next, when you do become aware of an intuitive hit, either follow it immediately or write it down for full consideration. Some intuitive hits are instructions to do something now, while others are big ideas that you will need to build over time.
>
> Write down your ideas and intuitive hits and the action you plan to take as a result. There is space in your Daily Action Log for you to capture these each day.
>
> Finally, go back through your notes weekly to make sure you've followed through on the intuitive hits as planned.

You Are Accountable to YOU!

The idea of accountability is one that seems to make some people nervous. Maybe they formed a negative association with the word from some movie where the gruff chief of police screamed at the detective, "If anything goes wrong, I'll hold you accountable!" Or, maybe they had a boss somewhere along the way who shouted the same thing at them. Thankfully, in this case, you are accountable only to yourself.

Ultimately, you are your own toughest critic. If you can keep yourself accountable to you, for the things that you decide you will do, you will achieve results that extend beyond your personal satisfaction and will be positively noticed by others. If your boss has given you an assignment, realize that your personal standard of excellence has the potential (if you choose) to extend way beyond his or hers.

Accountability and responsibility go hand in hand. Those of us who are responsible people are more than willing to be accountable as well. We'll do what it takes to get the job done well, not because someone else asked us to but because we believe in the job assigned and are responsible for upholding our personal standard of excellence.

To help you understand how to tap into resources that can help you be accountable to yourself and move closer to achieving your goals, I've included discussions about personal accountability, accountability partners and coaches, and mastermind teams.

Note to Business Leaders

Every business has a boss. In traditional "command and control" organizations, it is easy for employees to respond to the boss's wishes without question, engagement, or personal ownership.

As a business leader, recognize that you can develop your team's ownership and accountability by how you interact with them. By engaging them in your vision, sharing your goals for the team, and outlining the steps for pursuing those goals (the action plans), you will increase their involvement and find that they begin to hold you and their peers accountable for higher levels of performance.

It's exciting to see a team develop this level of accountability!

Personal Accountability

It's one thing to know what to do. It's another to actually do what needs to be done. The idea of personal accountability is that we do what it takes to be successful. We pledge each day to take action toward our most important goals and keep our commitments (even when nobody is looking).

Accountability is more than the results we achieve—it's also how we play the game. Are we following the processes we should be following, those that we know will get us to our goals faster? Are we acting from a place of integrity? Are we being genuine with the people around us?

This daily log was created to help you maintain a high level of personal accountability. Why? Because even the most committed and dedicated people tend to slip on occasion and forget to do some of those things they know will help them reach their goals. From personal experience, I know this daily log helps to keep people on track.

Want to make a fun game of your personal accountability? Decide what celebrations you will allow yourself when you complete your goals or milestones (sub-goals) along the way. Because celebrating is fun, there is a "muscle memory" created when you hit your goals and milestones. You want to repeat the feeling of success, partly because of the celebration. Find ways to enjoy the process of winning and create excuses to celebrate.

Your Action—Personal Accountability

Recognize that you are the one who will do the work to achieve your goals, and that you are happy to get into action to see your desired results.

Decide on a small celebration for your next goal or milestone. Your celebration can be as simple as taking a day off, buying yourself something you want, or going out to a nice dinner.

Review your Daily Action Log weekly and ask yourself, "What would I be willing to try differently to be even more accountable for my results?" Then, try the ideas that come up during the next two weeks. The Daily Action Log has a weekly score. What can you do to follow the suggestions in this book and raise your score?

The Role of Accountability Partners and Coaches

Beyond keeping the pages of this Daily Action Log updated, you may choose to use an accountability partner or hire a coach to play this role. An accountability partner is someone to help keep you accountable to the goals and actions that you decide are important to you.

Interestingly, many people want to achieve great results, commit to take action, and have the best intentions, only to slowly lose momentum and fall into old habits and miss their goals. How many people make New Year's resolutions, but by February they're a thing of the past? They are no longer committed to them.

When we keep to ourselves what it is that we've committed to do, we can easily talk ourselves out of doing what it takes. But what if we upped our game and shared our goals and planned actions with someone else, someone who agrees to keep us on track? Now it's a lot more difficult to let ourselves off the hook.

Accountability partners are non-judgmental. Their role is to hold you to what you say you're going to do, not evaluate your goals or planned actions, although if you ask them to they can be a great source of feedback and inspiration. What they will do is encourage you, share their observations, and give you the occasional nudge in the right direction.

For example, your accountability partner may say, "I noticed you only completed half your list of planned actions each of these last few days—what do you think that's about?" Or, "Do you have some resistance to number three on your list? It has been on your daily list every day for a week but you're not making progress on it." And encourage you by saying, "You can do this—what help do you need?"

You can ask someone to hold you accountable on a specific topic or across the full range of what you plan to do each day. Your accountability partner should be empowered to call you out when you don't do what you say you will.

> **Note to Business Leaders**
>
> I suggest to my business clients that they select accountability partners to help them keep on track for the metrics, targets, and action plans that are defined during the Strategic Goal Deployment™ process.
>
> Additionally, business leaders often benefit from having a coaching relationship that includes an accountability role. Should you decide to work with a coach, contact our office. You'll find it's a great way to accelerate your results.

If you choose to use an accountability partner across the full range of what you plan to do each day, it will help if they know your goals, not just what actions you plan to take tomorrow. Have a discussion once a month about your longer-term goals and then your specific focus for the month. Then, follow a format that is similar to the Daily Action Log pages in this book. You might find it easiest if you both have your own copy of this Daily Action Log so you can progress together at the same pace.

Using this Daily Action Log with your accountability partner will help you stay on track. I suggest your daily conversation follow this format:

You:

- "Here are all the daily habits I followed yesterday…"

- "Here are the planned actions I said I would complete… and here's what I did…"

- "Here are the insights and intuitive hits I received, and the inspired actions as a result…"

Your accountability partner (or coach):

- "Great job! Here's what I'm observing…"

- "A few questions I have are…"

Then, switch.

If you desire, you can ask for feedback and get into discussions to problem solve any issues you have. However, if you plan for a daily ten-minute call and they start to routinely take thirty minutes, you risk becoming frustrated by the time required. In my experience, these calls can be effective in just five to ten minutes.

You're forming a purposeful relationship around accountability, so you get to decide how you want to play—just make sure you both agree to the guidelines including duration and that the routine is benefiting both of you.

A coach and an accountability partner differ in that a coach is trained to recognize behavior patterns and can help you navigate through challenging situations. A coach can help you build success skills and break through barriers. When a coach plays the role of accountability partner for you, you can truly maximize your results and meet your potential.

> **Your Action—Accountability Partner**
>
> Ask someone to play the role of accountability partner for you as you strive to achieve your goals over the next ninety days. Ideally, it will be someone who is also following this same system and for whom you can reciprocate the role of accountability partner. Should you want extra help from a professional results coach trained in this process, refer to the contact information on page 185—Get Additional Help.
>
> Commit to staying with it during the next ninety days.

Mastermind Teams

The concept of masterminding has been in practice by the super-successful for years. In *Think and Grow Rich*, Napoleon Hill described how Henry Ford, Franklin Roosevelt, Harvey Firestone, John Burroughs, Luther Burbank, and others used masterminding to help grow their business empires and achieve great levels of success.[15]

A mastermind team is a group of people who get together periodically in person or via phone (or Skype) to help each other reach their goals. Imagine meeting with five or six people who all have goals and levels of success at or above your level along with a variety of backgrounds and experiences. Can you imagine how helpful they would be when you present a challenge or issue or want feedback about an idea? That's the essence of masterminding!

Mastermind teams are structured to maximize their effectiveness. This structure includes a strict agenda where, after an invocation to invite the ultimate mastermind team member (God, Higher Power, the Divine, Infinite Intelligence—you choose the name that fits with your beliefs), every member shares what's new and good, gets help with an issue, expresses gratitude, and makes a commitment to some stretch action prior to the next meeting. Roles rotate and include a leader, time keeper, and note taker.

The mastermind team members' contributions toward helping each other with their issues are amazing, especially because of the varied backgrounds and experience of the contributors. Additionally, advice for one team member will often serve the other members as well.

It's exciting to see the team members' successes, which tend to build momentum for the rest of the team. What helps drive us toward these great successes? The commitment to action that each member has is unwavering! Becoming involved in a well-structured and high-functioning mastermind team is an effective way to achieve your goals.

Can you see how this Daily Action Log can be a useful organizing tool to help you and your mastermind team drive the most important actions? As you receive insights and new ideas, turn them into inspired actions by writing them on the Daily Log sheets.

Your Action—Mastermind Team

If you already have a mastermind team, tell your team members about your commitment to follow this process for the next ninety days, and ask for their support.

If you don't yet have a mastermind team, consider five or six people who would be perfect for your team and ask them to form one with you. Decide on a schedule and begin your mastermind meetings.

Bonus action: Read chapter 46 of *The Success Principles* by Jack Canfield to learn more about mastermind teams.

---

* * *

Now that you've reviewed the basics of daily action, let's apply the three types of action to the Daily Action Log.

Affirmations

For each of your ninety-day goals, write an affirmation that describes you experiencing that goal complete. See the affirmation guidelines in chapter 2.

I am _____ly _____ing...
(feeling)   *(action)*

Financial

_____

_____

_____

Business/Career

_____

_____

_____

Health/Fitness

_____

_____

_____

Relationships

_____

_____

_____

Overall Happiness

_____

_____

_____

Download this template in convenient 8.5" x 11" size at
www.DailyActionLog.com

CHAPTER 3

How to Use
This Daily Action Log

Familiarize yourself with the layout of the Daily Action Log pages before you begin using it. This chapter will help you to get comfortable with the layout and understand how you'll use your Daily Action Log to keep the momentum of daily action toward your goals.

There are two page layouts: one that is used for every day of the week and one for the weekly summary. There are thirteen weeks of log pages here for you, as thirteen weeks covers ninety days (ninety-one, actually), or one quarter of the year. When you finish this ninety-day time period, you can start from the beginning with a new set of goals to achieve during the next quarter year.

You'll notice that the pages follow a pattern:

- Every Monday, you have the challenge of the week to help motivate you.

- Each Tuesday, Thursday, and Saturday you have an inspirational or thought-provoking quote.

- Every Wednesday, there is a fun fact for you.

- Every Friday, you will have a tip of the week.

- Sundays bring you a powerful success resource.

- Finally, each weekly summary provides a word of guidance from me, Pete Winiarski.

These are inspirational bonuses for you each day as you write in your Daily Action Log.

The Daily Action Log Sheet

The Daily Action Log sheets provide space to document many of the habits and principles that were described earlier in this book. The topics will be familiar to you now that you've read chapter 2, "The Basics of Daily Action."

The first section is where you write your *Intentions for Today*. Here's your chance to design your life and your experiences the way you want.

Next, there are a number of *Daily Habits* for you to implement. Remember, daily habits are one of the three types of action I described earlier, and are as important as the planned actions and inspired actions. These habits act as goal accelerators, so take them seriously.

In the next section, you have space for the *Five Daily Planned Actions*. You can write five actions that you plan to take today; these actions should be core actions that align with your goals, not superfluous busy work that isn't going to get you closer to completing your goals.

For example, I would not include responding to e-mails or surfing Facebook in your five daily planned actions. However, if there's an important e-mail from a contact regarding one of your specific goals, responding to that e-mail might make the list. Similarly, if your action plan for one of your goals includes e-mail marketing, then writing copy for your e-mail campaign or Facebook post could be a valid item to include on your list.

Next, there is space for you to capture any *Inspired Actions* that unexpectedly pop into your awareness as exciting intuitive hits or ideas that will help you move forward faster. Write them down here, and be sure to follow through!

Last, there is space for *Today's Lessons and Insights*. Here, record anything that is useful for you to track and remember. These notes could serve as helpful guideposts and prevent you from learning the same lessons the hard way, over and over again. For example, "I seem to have resistance to calling Bob; I didn't do it three days in a row." Or, "Getting up at 5:30 a.m. made all the difference!"

Check Boxes

You'll notice that in the Daily Habits and Five Daily Actions sections, there are a number of check boxes. Your task here is to complete what is listed and then place a check in the box next to that item. For example, if you visualized your goals as complete in the morning and again in the evening, you can check those two boxes, AM and PM, to give yourself credit for having followed through on that habit at the recommended times. Or, if you appreciated someone else, but not yourself, then you can check the one box but not the other.

With Five Daily Actions, check the box next to each that you complete. For example, if you said you would call and speak to Jim about his proposal, and you did indeed speak to Jim, place a check in that box. If you didn't complete one of the items, don't check the box for that item. Simple, right?

Your Action—Daily Action Log

Take a few moments to become familiar with the layout of the Daily Log Sheet.

The Weekly Summary Sheet

The Weekly Summary sheet contains three sections: *Tally of Last Week's Check Marks, Last Week's Insights,* and *Next Week's Goals.*

Tally of Last Week's Check Marks

Tally of Last Week's Check Marks is where you simply count up all the check marks beside the Daily Habits and Five Daily Planned Actions sections from Monday through Sunday this week. Each category has its own space to capture the number of check marks.

For example, every day you had two opportunities for check marks for "visualize goals as complete," one in the morning (AM) and one in the evening (PM). If you did this habit twice a day for all seven days, you would count fourteen check marks. Write this total in the space provided.

Next, count the number of check marks each day for the Five Daily Planned Actions. You would have the opportunity for five each day, times seven days, so thirty-five total check marks in this area.

Now, add the total number of check marks and write it in the total box to the right of the blank spaces for each individual category. You'll note it says, "This Week's Total Score." This number is out of a total of 119 possible check marks.

The real value of the number of check marks is to provide feedback about how much you did this week. The goal is *not* necessarily to get 119 points. Having fun with the process and meeting your goals on time or early is more important than your total number of check marks. Notice how many points you have, but also notice how you did toward achieving your goals and how satisfied you feel about your progress.

Now, I know how competitive some of you are and maybe getting close to 119 is important to you—if so, that's okay, too. Just don't lose sight of the larger goals you set out to achieve in the first place.

Also notice if you have a low point total in one area. For example, maybe you have zero for reading. That's interesting feedback for you. Based on that score, what do you choose to do next week? The best part is that nobody says you must read (although research suggests it will help you achieve your goals faster), you get to decide if you want to. Assuming you do want to read every day but have zero points, that's useful to recognize, isn't it?

Interesting Feedback Indeed!

Here is the check-mark tally from my first two weeks using the Daily Action Log. You'll notice a few things when you study my first week results. First, I scored only thirty-five out of 119. I had zero in four categories. I had only fourteen of my five daily actions (out of thirty-five possible) complete. This is great feedback!

	First Week	Second Week	Possible
Daily Habits:			
Visualize Goals as Complete	0	12	14
Say Affirmations for Goals	2	11	14
Appreciation/Gratitude	0	11	14
Meditate	5	6	7
Read	5	6	7
Exercise	6	6	7
"Letting Go"	0	2	7
Journal	3	5	7
Optional Habit	0	1	7
Five Daily Actions:	14	21	35
This Week's Total Score	35	81	119

I share this because even though I've done every one of these practices from time to time, clearly I had fallen away from some of these habits. I also want you to know that even the author got off to a slow start using this tool. Remember, the purpose is to achieve your ninety-day goals, not to get a perfect score of 119. Even though at one week into this process I had a low score, I have plenty of time to recover and have some ideas of where to place a little more effort. See if you can beat my first week's score!

With the insights this first week provided, I invested some time to write my goals and affirmations on 3" x 5" index cards to make it easier to visualize and affirm my goals. I made appreciation a priority. And, I had better progress on my five daily planned actions. Notice that my second week scored much higher at eighty-one!

Last Week's Insights

In the section called *Last Week's Insights*, you have an opportunity to write a few lines about your experience this week. Describe how you're doing and what you might do differently. Write any lessons you want to carry forward as a wiser version of you for next week. Congratulate yourself where things worked great. This is also where your point totals for each category may have a story to tell. What are they saying to you?

Next Week's Goals

Finally, you have a place to write *Next Week's Goals*. These are smaller goals that feed the main goals you set for this ninety-day period. The reason you set the goals for the next week now (rather than all thirteen weeks in advance) is that you'll experience more success if you have the clearest possible picture of where you are at the beginning of the week, and a realistic but aggressive assessment of what you will strive to attain this week. Naturally, if you make great progress on your weekly goals, you should feel like you've made a great step forward toward your ninety-day goals, too.

Also, it's rare we're *exactly* on schedule. We're usually ahead or behind, even if by just a small amount. Your weekly goals allow you to target your actions to where you are right now.

To illustrate how goals align, let's say that one of your ninety-day goals is to write a book. Your goal for the week might be to create a first draft of forty pages. If you decide that you will write five days next week, you will need to be sure to write eight pages minimum on each of those five days in order to cover your projected forty pages. Your goal for the week is clear, and this should feed your daily planned actions.

Let's say that you are in a sales role and a ninety-day goal you have is to confirm two major contracts. During the ninety days, you will need to do some prospecting, sales presentations, follow-up, and close the sales. Your goal for the week might be to confirm five appointments for you to share your sales presentation. Your daily actions might include the number of calls you will make in order to confirm the appointments. You can see that confirming the appointments will lead to the presentations, which will in turn lead to closing sales and ultimately reaching your goal of booking two major contracts.

Think of completing the Weekly Summary Sheet as giving you a clean slate to move into the next week, fresh and energized to accomplish your goals!

> **Your Action—Weekly Summary Sheet**
>
> Take a few moments to become familiar with the layout of the Weekly Summary sheet.

Eight Things to Consider When Completing the Check Boxes for the Day

1. **Prioritize achieving the goals that you defined, *ahead of* getting a lot of check marks.** Having said that, the check marks can help ensure you stay disciplined in following the daily habits, defining five meaningful actions to take each day, and being open to intuitive hits that may lead to inspired actions. Do this on a regular basis and you will complete the goals you set out.

2. **Budget your time wisely.** If today is a normal day for you and you can afford an hour to complete all the daily habits before you shower and get into the rest of your day, go for it! If you have to get up ninety minutes earlier than normal to zip to the airport for an early flight and the day is full of travel, you may decide to do some of the habits on the plane rather than before your shower. Do what works for you.

3. **Keep your commitments.** If you make a commitment to complete an action, make sure you complete that action. If you have to do another thirty minutes of work after the kids go to bed in order to keep your commitments, do it.

4. **Commit to what you have the capacity to do.** This means that you have to be honest with yourself about your to-do list. If you find that you're regularly staying up late to finish what you committed to complete, you may want to make a few changes to the size of your to-do list or at least when you will tackle the items.

5. **Remember that every day is an experiment and opportunity to learn.** If you find you can't easily keep all your commitments, ponder why that might be, consider the lesson or insight, and capture this in your log. You might discover that you feel bulletproof when you do your daily habits in the morning. You may realize that you are most productive right before lunch (or in the evening, or early morning). Try different routines and see what works best for you.

6. Have fun. Achieving your goals, no matter how challenging they are, is meant to be fun, exciting, and downright exhilarating! The Daily Action Log is designed to help you get there by following proven principles. If you're not having fun, you're probably not doing it right.

7. Think ahead. If you're like many others, this process will help you to blow away your goals! You'll get them completed faster than you ever thought possible. Consider your goals for the subsequent ninety days and be prepared to get a jump on them.

8. Be flexible with what life throws at you. Just as you may be thrilled to find everything went faster than you imagined it would, you may also find that other surprises pop up and knock you off track. If this happens, get up as soon as you can and keep moving. If you need to attend to some unforeseen emergency, renegotiate your goals (with yourself and share with your accountability partner or coach) and take care of business. Then, come back with renewed vigor. The good news about this process is that you can still use it during the time you're handling the unforeseen emergency—just alter the five daily actions to align with your most pressing issues until you're ready to come back to your original goals.

* * *

Now that you know how to use this Daily Action Log, refer to the daily and weekly sample pages that follow, and let's get started!

Sample Daily Log Sheet

Intentions for Today:

Confirm client will start before end of month.

Daily Habits:

Visualize Goals as Complete		AM ☑	PM ☐	
Say Affirmations for Goals		AM ☑	PM ☐	
Express Appreciation/Gratitude		Self ☑	Someone Else ☑	

Meditate ☑ Notes: Morning — 15 min.

Read ☑ Notes: 1 chapter of Think and Grow Rich

Exercise ☑ Notes: 20 min on bike

"Letting Go" ☑ Method: Ho'oponopono

Journal ☑ Notes: after meditating

Optional Habit ☑ Notes: 10 glasses of water

Five Daily Planned Actions:

1. Call client to confirm start date ☑
2. Create 1st draft of kick-off presentation ☑
3. Review Strategic Plan ☑
4. Respond to Joe's email question ☐
5. Edit website copy ☑

Inspired Actions:

Idea for solving Joe's problem — accelerate product release by 30 days = $200k savings.

Today's Lessons and Insights:

Easy to drink lots of water when exercise in morning.

Sample Weekly Summary Sheet

Tally of Last Week's Check Marks:

Daily Habits:

Visualize Goals as Complete	8	/14
Say Affirmations for Goals	10	/14
Appreciation/Gratitude	11	/14
Meditate	5	/ 7
Read	4	/ 7
Exercise	2	/ 7
"Letting Go"	3	/ 7
Journal	5	/ 7
Optional Habit	3	/ 7
Five Daily Actions:	19	/35

This Week's Total Score

70

Out of 119

Last Week's Insights:

- Exercise in morning — easy to drink lots of water plus had more energy those days
- I was resisting calling Joe because I wasn't sure how to answer his question — meditation gave me great insight
- Busy week — exercise suffered

Next Week's Goals:

1. Complete kick-off presentation
2. Contact 3 people from network mtg / arrange calls
3. Send website edits to developer
4. Plan team feedback sessions — New Process
5. Write job spec and have HR begin recruiting

Weekly Success Tips

1. **Visualize and affirm first thing in the morning and right before bed.** When you first wake, visualize and affirm your goals while your brain is still in alpha state, as this will help your creativity and learning. Also, what you experience during the last thirty minutes before you fall asleep replays in your unconscious mind during the night.

2. **Build in an exercise routine.** Exercise gives you energy to take on all your other projects. Plus, what you learn in hitting your exercise goals translates to your other goals.

3. **Enjoy the process every step of the way.** Success and goal achievement is not just about the end result. It's about the journey and who you become through the process.

4. **Include many small goals that add up to a big goal.** It's okay to set a big goal but include smaller sub-goals to help you keep momentum.

5. **Set at least one breakthrough goal.** Think of what would really change the game for you and rocket you forward!

6. **Celebrate every win, big and small.** Celebrating helps you build "muscle memory" and create a natural desire to repeat the activity and outcome that led to the celebration.

7. **Ask for help.** Success is a team sport. If you get help from others along the way you'll get better results, faster. Remember, even the world's top athletes have coaches to help them improve their performance. You can, too.

8. **Help other people achieve their goals.** You'll feel good, you might learn something, you'll strengthen your network, and it's simply a darn good thing to do.

9. **Schedule time in your calendar for your goal-related actions.** Control your calendar. Fill it with what you think is important to work on—your daily habits and your five daily planned actions—and let everything else fill in around it.

10. **Start your day with one of the daily habits.** It's easier to do them before other distractions prevent you from getting started.

11. **Take at least one day off each week.** It's okay to give yourself some breathing space. The whole process should be fun, remember?

12. **Be honest about what's working and what isn't.** We're all different. Discover what works best for you, and do more of it. If something isn't working, assess why and learn from it. Then, decide what you will do going forward.

13. **Trust the process and keep at it.** Following these methods will help you achieve the results you want. Believe they'll work and they will. At the same time, know you're exactly where you're supposed to be, so if your results don't match your expectations, there's a reason; assess the feedback from the Daily Action Log and determine whether changes are necessary.

Challenge of the Week

I have found that adding a specific challenge each week helps to spice things up. Here is a list of the challenges that I've included each week. See if you can rise to the challenge and increase your progress rate!

1. Go on a walk (or run, or bike ride) for at least an hour once this week.

2. Finish your five planned actions before lunch every day this week.

3. Visualize your goals and say your affirmations three times every day this week—morning, noon, and night.

4. Meditate at least once a day this week.

5. Listen to your intuition, and follow through on your intuitive hits within twenty-four hours each day this week.

6. Send a note of appreciation and gratitude to a different person every day this week.

7. Take at least ten minutes each day this week to journal and capture as many ideas as possible.

8. Set your alarm an hour earlier than normal every day this week to get a head start on your day.

9. Try a new method of Letting Go this week, and consciously practice it on an issue every day.

10. Every evening this week before bed, look in the mirror and tell yourself how much you appreciate your efforts; emphasize the positive.

11. Choose at least one book to read cover to cover this week.

12. Eliminate television from your life every day this week (yes, including the weekend) and replace that time with action on your goals (daily habits, planned actions, or inspired actions).

13. Find at least one success to celebrate this week, and include other people in your celebration—let them know about your success.

Your Daily
Action Log

The Daily Action Log sheets and the other forms used throughout *Act Now!* can be downloaded in convenient 8.5" x 11" size from www.DailyActionLog.com

> **Challenge of the week:** *Go on a walk (or run, or bike ride) for at least an hour once this week.*

Monday   Date: _____

Intentions for Today:

Daily Habits:

Visualize Goals as Complete	AM ☐ PM ☐
Say Affirmations for Goals	AM ☐ PM ☐
Express Appreciation/Gratitude	Self ☐ Someone Else ☐

Meditate ☐ Notes: _____

Read ☐ Notes: _____

Exercise ☐ Notes: _____

"Letting Go" ☐ Method: _____

Journal ☐ Notes: _____

Optional Habit ☐ Notes: _____

Five Daily Planned Actions:

1. _____ ☐

2. _____ ☐

3. _____ ☐

4. _____ ☐

5. _____ ☐

Inspired Actions:

Today's Lessons and Insights:

> *"Our greatest glory is not in never falling, but in rising every time we fall."*
> ~ *Confucius*

Tuesday   Date: _____

Intentions for Today:

Daily Habits:

Visualize Goals as Complete   AM ☐   PM ☐
Say Affirmations for Goals   AM ☐   PM ☐
Express Appreciation/Gratitude   Self ☐   Someone Else ☐

Meditate   ☐   Notes: _____
Read   ☐   Notes: _____
Exercise   ☐   Notes: _____
"Letting Go"   ☐   Method: _____
Journal   ☐   Notes: _____
Optional Habit   ☐   Notes: _____

Five Daily Planned Actions:

1. _____ ☐
2. _____ ☐
3. _____ ☐
4. _____ ☐
5. _____ ☐

Inspired Actions:

Today's Lessons and Insights:

Wednesday

Date: _____

Intentions for Today:

Daily Habits:

Visualize Goals as Complete	AM ☐	PM ☐
Say Affirmations for Goals	AM ☐	PM ☐
Express Appreciation/Gratitude	Self ☐	Someone Else ☐

Meditate ☐ Notes: _____

Read ☐ Notes: _____

Exercise ☐ Notes: _____

"Letting Go" ☐ Method: _____

Journal ☐ Notes: _____

Optional Habit ☐ Notes: _____

Five Daily Planned Actions:

1. _____ ☐

2. _____ ☐

3. _____ ☐

4. _____ ☐

5. _____ ☐

Inspired Actions:

Today's Lessons and Insights:

> *"If you are going to achieve a goal, you first have to believe it's possible, and then you have to believe it's possible for you, not just for other people"*   *~ Jack Canfield*

Thursday

Date: _____

Intentions for Today:

Daily Habits:

Visualize Goals as Complete	AM ☐	PM ☐
Say Affirmations for Goals	AM ☐	PM ☐
Express Appreciation/Gratitude	Self ☐	Someone Else ☐

Meditate ☐ Notes: _____

Read ☐ Notes: _____

Exercise ☐ Notes: _____

"Letting Go" ☐ Method: _____

Journal ☐ Notes: _____

Optional Habit ☐ Notes: _____

Five Daily Planned Actions:

1. _____ ☐
2. _____ ☐
3. _____ ☐
4. _____ ☐
5. _____ ☐

Inspired Actions:

Today's Lessons and Insights:

Friday

Date: _____

Intentions for Today:

Daily Habits:

Visualize Goals as Complete	AM ☐	PM ☐
Say Affirmations for Goals	AM ☐	PM ☐
Express Appreciation/Gratitude	Self ☐	Someone Else ☐

Meditate ☐ Notes: _____

Read ☐ Notes: _____

Exercise ☐ Notes: _____

"Letting Go" ☐ Method: _____

Journal ☐ Notes: _____

Optional Habit ☐ Notes: _____

Five Daily Planned Actions:

1. _____ ☐

2. _____ ☐

3. _____ ☐

4. _____ ☐

5. _____ ☐

Inspired Actions:

Today's Lessons and Insights:

"You don't get what you want or wish for in life; you'll always get what you're prepared to attract."
~ Sean Smith

Saturday

Date: _____

Intentions for Today:

Daily Habits:

Visualize Goals as Complete   AM ☐   PM ☐

Say Affirmations for Goals   AM ☐   PM ☐

Express Appreciation/Gratitude   Self ☐   Someone Else ☐

Meditate   ☐   Notes: _____

Read   ☐   Notes: _____

Exercise   ☐   Notes: _____

"Letting Go"   ☐   Method: _____

Journal   ☐   Notes: _____

Optional Habit   ☐   Notes: _____

Five Daily Planned Actions:

1. _____ ☐

2. _____ ☐

3. _____ ☐

4. _____ ☐

5. _____ ☐

Inspired Actions:

Today's Lessons and Insights:

Sunday

Date: _____

Intentions for Today:

Daily Habits:

Visualize Goals as Complete	AM ☐	PM ☐
Say Affirmations for Goals	AM ☐	PM ☐
Express Appreciation/Gratitude	Self ☐	Someone Else ☐

Meditate ☐ Notes: _____

Read ☐ Notes: _____

Exercise ☐ Notes: _____

"Letting Go" ☐ Method: _____

Journal ☐ Notes: _____

Optional Habit ☐ Notes: _____

Five Daily Planned Actions:

1. _____ ☐

2. _____ ☐

3. _____ ☐

4. _____ ☐

5. _____ ☐

Inspired Actions:

Today's Lessons and Insights:

"If you are clear what the highest leverage actions are, start there."

~ *Pete Winiarski*

Weekly Summary   Week 1

Tally of Last Week's Check Marks:

Daily Habits:

Visualize Goals as Complete	_____ / 14
Say Affirmations for Goals	_____ / 14
Appreciation/ Gratitude	_____ / 14
Meditate	_____ / 7
Read	_____ / 7
Exercise	_____ / 7
"Letting Go"	_____ / 7
Journal	_____ / 7
Optional Habit	_____ / 7
Five Daily Actions:	_____ / 35

This Week's Total Score

Out of 119

Last Week's Insights:

_____

_____

_____

_____

_____

Next Week's Goals:

_____

_____

_____

_____

_____

Challenge of the week: *Finish your five planned actions before lunch every day this week.*

Monday

Date: _____

Intentions for Today:

Daily Habits:

Visualize Goals as Complete	AM ☐	PM ☐
Say Affirmations for Goals	AM ☐	PM ☐
Express Appreciation/Gratitude	Self ☐	Someone Else ☐

Meditate ☐ Notes: _____

Read ☐ Notes: _____

Exercise ☐ Notes: _____

"Letting Go" ☐ Method: _____

Journal ☐ Notes: _____

Optional Habit ☐ Notes: _____

Five Daily Planned Actions:

1. _____ ☐

2. _____ ☐

3. _____ ☐

4. _____ ☐

5. _____ ☐

Inspired Actions:

Today's Lessons and Insights:

> *"The ability to convert ideas to things is the secret to outward success."*
> ~ *Henry Ward Beecher*

Tuesday

Date: _____

Intentions for Today:

Daily Habits:

Visualize Goals as Complete	AM ☐	PM ☐
Say Affirmations for Goals	AM ☐	PM ☐
Express Appreciation/Gratitude	Self ☐	Someone Else ☐

Meditate ☐ Notes: _____

Read ☐ Notes: _____

Exercise ☐ Notes: _____

"Letting Go" ☐ Method: _____

Journal ☐ Notes: _____

Optional Habit ☐ Notes: _____

Five Daily Planned Actions:

1. _____ ☐

2. _____ ☐

3. _____ ☐

4. _____ ☐

5. _____ ☐

Inspired Actions:

Today's Lessons and Insights:

Fun fact: *If you read a half-hour a day it is equivalent to taking five college courses each year.*

Wednesday

Date: _____

Intentions for Today:

Daily Habits:

Visualize Goals as Complete	AM ☐	PM ☐
Say Affirmations for Goals	AM ☐	PM ☐
Express Appreciation/Gratitude	Self ☐	Someone Else ☐

Meditate ☐ Notes: _____

Read ☐ Notes: _____

Exercise ☐ Notes: _____

"Letting Go" ☐ Method: _____

Journal ☐ Notes: _____

Optional Habit ☐ Notes: _____

Five Daily Planned Actions:

1. _____ ☐
2. _____ ☐
3. _____ ☐
4. _____ ☐
5. _____ ☐

Inspired Actions:

Today's Lessons and Insights:

> *"It is not enough to take steps which may someday lead to a goal; each step must be itself a goal and a step likewise."*
> ~ *Johann Wolfgang von Goethe*

Thursday

Date: _____

Intentions for Today:

Daily Habits:

Visualize Goals as Complete	AM ☐ PM ☐
Say Affirmations for Goals	AM ☐ PM ☐
Express Appreciation/Gratitude	Self ☐ Someone Else ☐

Meditate ☐ Notes: _____

Read ☐ Notes: _____

Exercise ☐ Notes: _____

"Letting Go" ☐ Method: _____

Journal ☐ Notes: _____

Optional Habit ☐ Notes: _____

Five Daily Planned Actions:

1. _____ ☐

2. _____ ☐

3. _____ ☐

4. _____ ☐

5. _____ ☐

Inspired Actions:

Today's Lessons and Insights:

Tip of the week: *Build an exercise routine into your schedule—get your body moving!*

Friday

Date: _____

Intentions for Today:

Daily Habits:

Visualize Goals as Complete	AM ☐	PM ☐
Say Affirmations for Goals	AM ☐	PM ☐
Express Appreciation/Gratitude	Self ☐	Someone Else ☐

Meditate ☐ Notes: _____

Read ☐ Notes: _____

Exercise ☐ Notes: _____

"Letting Go" ☐ Method: _____

Journal ☐ Notes: _____

Optional Habit ☐ Notes: _____

Five Daily Planned Actions:

1. _____ ☐

2. _____ ☐

3. _____ ☐

4. _____ ☐

5. _____ ☐

Inspired Actions:

Today's Lessons and Insights:

> *"The only thing you need is an intention, and the will to enact it."*
>
> ~ Deidre Hade

Saturday

Date: _____

Intentions for Today:

Daily Habits:

Visualize Goals as Complete	AM ☐ PM ☐
Say Affirmations for Goals	AM ☐ PM ☐
Express Appreciation/Gratitude	Self ☐ Someone Else ☐

Meditate ☐ Notes: _____

Read ☐ Notes: _____

Exercise ☐ Notes: _____

"Letting Go" ☐ Method: _____

Journal ☐ Notes: _____

Optional Habit ☐ Notes: _____

Five Daily Planned Actions:

1. _____ ☐

2. _____ ☐

3. _____ ☐

4. _____ ☐

5. _____ ☐

Inspired Actions:

Today's Lessons and Insights:

Powerful success resources: *Jack Canfield's The Success Principles. A must read to understand your success potential more deeply.*

Sunday

Date: _____

Intentions for Today:

Daily Habits:

Visualize Goals as Complete	AM ☐	PM ☐
Say Affirmations for Goals	AM ☐	PM ☐
Express Appreciation/Gratitude	Self ☐	Someone Else ☐

Meditate ☐ Notes: _____

Read ☐ Notes: _____

Exercise ☐ Notes: _____

"Letting Go" ☐ Method: _____

Journal ☐ Notes: _____

Optional Habit ☐ Notes: _____

Five Daily Planned Actions:

1. _____ ☐

2. _____ ☐

3. _____ ☐

4. _____ ☐

5. _____ ☐

Inspired Actions:

Today's Lessons and Insights:

> *"If you're not having fun, you're not doing it right."*
>
> ~ *Pete Winiarski*

Weekly Summary   Week 2

Tally of Last Week's Check Marks:

Daily Habits:

Visualize Goals as Complete	_____ / 14	
Say Affirmations for Goals	_____ / 14	
Appreciation/ Gratitude	_____ / 14	
Meditate	_____ / 7	
Read	_____ / 7	
Exercise	_____ / 7	
"Letting Go"	_____ / 7	
Journal	_____ / 7	
Optional Habit	_____ / 7	
Five Daily Actions:	_____ / 35	

This Week's Total Score

[ ]

Out of 119

Last Week's Insights:

_____

_____

_____

_____

_____

Next Week's Goals:

_____

_____

_____

_____

_____

> **Challenge of the week:** *Visualize your goals and say your affirmations three times every day this week—morning, noon, and night.*

Monday

Date: _____

Intentions for Today:

Daily Habits:

Visualize Goals as Complete   AM ☐   PM ☐

Say Affirmations for Goals   AM ☐   PM ☐

Express Appreciation/Gratitude   Self ☐   Someone Else ☐

Meditate	☐	Notes: _____
Read	☐	Notes: _____
Exercise	☐	Notes: _____
"Letting Go"	☐	Method: _____
Journal	☐	Notes: _____
Optional Habit	☐	Notes: _____

Five Daily Planned Actions:

1. _____ ☐
2. _____ ☐
3. _____ ☐
4. _____ ☐
5. _____ ☐

Inspired Actions:

Today's Lessons and Insights:

"Determine never to be idle…it is wonderful how much may be done if we are always doing."
~ Thomas Jefferson

Tuesday   Date: _____

Intentions for Today:

Daily Habits:

Visualize Goals as Complete   AM ☐   PM ☐

Say Affirmations for Goals   AM ☐   PM ☐

Express Appreciation/Gratitude   Self ☐   Someone Else ☐

Meditate   ☐   Notes: _____

Read   ☐   Notes: _____

Exercise   ☐   Notes: _____

"Letting Go"   ☐   Method: _____

Journal   ☐   Notes: _____

Optional Habit   ☐   Notes: _____

Five Daily Planned Actions:

1. _____ ☐

2. _____ ☐

3. _____ ☐

4. _____ ☐

5. _____ ☐

Inspired Actions:

Today's Lessons and Insights:

Wednesday

Date: _____

Intentions for Today:

Daily Habits:

Visualize Goals as Complete	AM ☐	PM ☐
Say Affirmations for Goals	AM ☐	PM ☐
Express Appreciation/Gratitude	Self ☐	Someone Else ☐

Meditate ☐ Notes: _____

Read ☐ Notes: _____

Exercise ☐ Notes: _____

"Letting Go" ☐ Method: _____

Journal ☐ Notes: _____

Optional Habit ☐ Notes: _____

Five Daily Planned Actions:

1. _____ ☐

2. _____ ☐

3. _____ ☐

4. _____ ☐

5. _____ ☐

Inspired Actions:

Today's Lessons and Insights:

> *"The constitution only guarantees the American people the right to pursue happiness. You have to catch it yourself."*
> *~ attributed to Benjamin Franklin*

Thursday

Date: _____

Intentions for Today:

Daily Habits:

Visualize Goals as Complete	AM ☐	PM ☐
Say Affirmations for Goals	AM ☐	PM ☐
Express Appreciation/Gratitude	Self ☐	Someone Else ☐

Meditate ☐ Notes: _____

Read ☐ Notes: _____

Exercise ☐ Notes: _____

"Letting Go" ☐ Method: _____

Journal ☐ Notes: _____

Optional Habit ☐ Notes: _____

Five Daily Planned Actions:

1. _____ ☐

2. _____ ☐

3. _____ ☐

4. _____ ☐

5. _____ ☐

Inspired Actions:

Today's Lessons and Insights:

Tip of the week: *Enjoy the process, every step of the way.*

Friday
Date: _____

Intentions for Today:

Daily Habits:

Visualize Goals as Complete	AM ☐	PM ☐
Say Affirmations for Goals	AM ☐	PM ☐
Express Appreciation/Gratitude	Self ☐	Someone Else ☐

Meditate ☐ Notes: _____

Read ☐ Notes: _____

Exercise ☐ Notes: _____

"Letting Go" ☐ Method: _____

Journal ☐ Notes: _____

Optional Habit ☐ Notes: _____

Five Daily Planned Actions:

1. _____ ☐

2. _____ ☐

3. _____ ☐

4. _____ ☐

5. _____ ☐

Inspired Actions:

Today's Lessons and Insights:

> *"Accountability, not ability, determines your results."*
>
> ~ *Tiffany Peterson*

Saturday

Date: _____

Intentions for Today:

Daily Habits:

Visualize Goals as Complete   AM ☐   PM ☐
Say Affirmations for Goals   AM ☐   PM ☐
Express Appreciation/Gratitude   Self ☐   Someone Else ☐

Meditate ☐   Notes: _____
Read ☐   Notes: _____
Exercise ☐   Notes: _____
"Letting Go" ☐   Method: _____
Journal ☐   Notes: _____
Optional Habit ☐ Notes: _____

Five Daily Planned Actions:

1. _____ ☐
2. _____ ☐
3. _____ ☐
4. _____ ☐
5. _____ ☐

Inspired Actions:

Today's Lessons and Insights:

> **Powerful success resources:** *The Field and The Intuition Experiment by Lynne McTaggart explain how quantum physics impacts our success and goal achievement..*

Sunday   Date: _____

Intentions for Today:

Daily Habits:

Visualize Goals as Complete		AM ☐	PM ☐
Say Affirmations for Goals		AM ☐	PM ☐
Express Appreciation/Gratitude		Self ☐	Someone Else ☐

Meditate	☐	Notes: _____
Read	☐	Notes: _____
Exercise	☐	Notes: _____
"Letting Go"	☐	Method: _____
Journal	☐	Notes: _____
Optional Habit	☐	Notes: _____

Five Daily Planned Actions:

1. _____ ☐
2. _____ ☐
3. _____ ☐
4. _____ ☐
5. _____ ☐

Inspired Actions:

Today's Lessons and Insights:

> *"It's okay to be considered successful by others, but be okay about yourself first."*
> ~ *Pete Winiarski*

Weekly Summary   Week 3

Tally of Last Week's Check Marks:

Daily Habits:

Visualize Goals as Complete	_____	/ 14
Say Affirmations for Goals	_____	/ 14
Appreciation/ Gratitude	_____	/ 14
Meditate	_____	/ 7
Read	_____	/ 7
Exercise	_____	/ 7
"Letting Go"	_____	/ 7
Journal	_____	/ 7
Optional Habit	_____	/ 7
Five Daily Actions:	_____	/ 35

This Week's Total Score

Out of 119

Last Week's Insights:

_____

_____

_____

_____

_____

Next Week's Goals:

_____

_____

_____

_____

_____

Challenge of the week: *Meditate at least once a day this week.*

Monday

Date: _____

Intentions for Today:

Daily Habits:

Visualize Goals as Complete   AM ☐   PM ☐

Say Affirmations for Goals   AM ☐   PM ☐

Express Appreciation/Gratitude   Self ☐   Someone Else ☐

Meditate	☐	Notes: _____
Read	☐	Notes: _____
Exercise	☐	Notes: _____
"Letting Go"	☐	Method: _____
Journal	☐	Notes: _____
Optional Habit	☐	Notes: _____

Five Daily Planned Actions:

1. _____ ☐
2. _____ ☐
3. _____ ☐
4. _____ ☐
5. _____ ☐

Inspired Actions:

Today's Lessons and Insights:

"In absence of clearly defined goals, we become strangely loyal to performing daily acts of trivia."
~ *Author unknown*

Tuesday

Date: _____

Intentions for Today:

Daily Habits:

Visualize Goals as Complete	AM ☐	PM ☐
Say Affirmations for Goals	AM ☐	PM ☐
Express Appreciation/Gratitude	Self ☐	Someone Else ☐

Meditate ☐ Notes: _____

Read ☐ Notes: _____

Exercise ☐ Notes: _____

"Letting Go" ☐ Method: _____

Journal ☐ Notes: _____

Optional Habit ☐ Notes: _____

Five Daily Planned Actions:

1. _____ ☐

2. _____ ☐

3. _____ ☐

4. _____ ☐

5. _____ ☐

Inspired Actions:

Today's Lessons and Insights:

Fun fact: *Repeating a goal out loud gives it a better opportunity to become reality.*

Wednesday

Date: _____

Intentions for Today:

Daily Habits:

Visualize Goals as Complete   AM ☐   PM ☐

Say Affirmations for Goals   AM ☐   PM ☐

Express Appreciation/Gratitude   Self ☐   Someone Else ☐

Meditate   ☐   Notes: _____

Read   ☐   Notes: _____

Exercise   ☐   Notes: _____

"Letting Go"   ☐   Method: _____

Journal   ☐   Notes: _____

Optional Habit   ☐   Notes: _____

Five Daily Planned Actions:

1. _____ ☐

2. _____ ☐

3. _____ ☐

4. _____ ☐

5. _____ ☐

Inspired Actions:

Today's Lessons and Insights:

> *"Most folks are about as happy as they make up their minds to be."*
>
> ~ *Abraham Lincoln*

Thursday

Date: _____

Intentions for Today:

Daily Habits:

Visualize Goals as Complete	AM ☐	PM ☐
Say Affirmations for Goals	AM ☐	PM ☐
Express Appreciation/Gratitude	Self ☐	Someone Else ☐

Meditate ☐ Notes: _____

Read ☐ Notes: _____

Exercise ☐ Notes: _____

"Letting Go" ☐ Method: _____

Journal ☐ Notes: _____

Optional Habit ☐ Notes: _____

Five Daily Planned Actions:

1. _____ ☐
2. _____ ☐
3. _____ ☐
4. _____ ☐
5. _____ ☐

Inspired Actions:

Today's Lessons and Insights:

Friday

Date: _____

Intentions for Today:

Daily Habits:

Visualize Goals as Complete	AM ☐ PM ☐
Say Affirmations for Goals	AM ☐ PM ☐
Express Appreciation/Gratitude	Self ☐ Someone Else ☐

Meditate ☐ Notes: _____

Read ☐ Notes: _____

Exercise ☐ Notes: _____

"Letting Go" ☐ Method: _____

Journal ☐ Notes: _____

Optional Habit ☐ Notes: _____

Five Daily Planned Actions:

1. _____ ☐
2. _____ ☐
3. _____ ☐
4. _____ ☐
5. _____ ☐

Inspired Actions:

Today's Lessons and Insights:

> *"A man has to have goals—for a day, for a lifetime—and that was mine, to have people say, 'There goes Ted Williams, the greatest hitter who ever lived.'"* ~ *Ted Williams*

Saturday

Date: _____

Intentions for Today:

Daily Habits:

Visualize Goals as Complete	AM ☐	PM ☐
Say Affirmations for Goals	AM ☐	PM ☐
Express Appreciation/Gratitude	Self ☐	Someone Else ☐

Meditate ☐ Notes: _____

Read ☐ Notes: _____

Exercise ☐ Notes: _____

"Letting Go" ☐ Method: _____

Journal ☐ Notes: _____

Optional Habit ☐ Notes: _____

Five Daily Planned Actions:

1. _____ ☐
2. _____ ☐
3. _____ ☐
4. _____ ☐
5. _____ ☐

Inspired Actions:

Today's Lessons and Insights:

> **Powerful success resources:** *Jim Bunch's The Ultimate Game of Life, www.UltimateGameInfo.com.*

Sunday

Date: _____

Intentions for Today:

Daily Habits:

Visualize Goals as Complete	AM ☐	PM ☐
Say Affirmations for Goals	AM ☐	PM ☐
Express Appreciation/Gratitude	Self ☐	Someone Else ☐

Meditate ☐ Notes: _____

Read ☐ Notes: _____

Exercise ☐ Notes: _____

"Letting Go" ☐ Method: _____

Journal ☐ Notes: _____

Optional Habit ☐ Notes: _____

Five Daily Planned Actions:

1. _____ ☐

2. _____ ☐

3. _____ ☐

4. _____ ☐

5. _____ ☐

Inspired Actions:

Today's Lessons and Insights:

> *"Now is a great time to start. Nothing will happen until you do."*
>
> ~ *Pete Winiarski*

Weekly Summary   Week 4

Tally of Last Week's Check Marks:

Daily Habits:

Visualize Goals as Complete	_____	/ 14
Say Affirmations for Goals	_____	/ 14
Appreciation/ Gratitude	_____	/ 14
Meditate	_____	/ 7
Read	_____	/ 7
Exercise	_____	/ 7
"Letting Go"	_____	/ 7
Journal	_____	/ 7
Optional Habit	_____	/ 7
Five Daily Actions:	_____	/ 35

This Week's Total Score

Out of 119

Last Week's Insights:

_____

_____

_____

_____

_____

Next Week's Goals:

_____

_____

_____

_____

_____

> **Challenge of the week:** *Listen to your intuition and follow through on your intuitive hits within twenty-four hours each day this week.*

Monday

Date: _____

Intentions for Today:

Daily Habits:

Visualize Goals as Complete	AM ☐	PM ☐
Say Affirmations for Goals	AM ☐	PM ☐
Express Appreciation/Gratitude	Self ☐	Someone Else ☐

Meditate	☐	Notes: _____
Read	☐	Notes: _____
Exercise	☐	Notes: _____
"Letting Go"	☐	Method: _____
Journal	☐	Notes: _____
Optional Habit	☐	Notes: _____

Five Daily Planned Actions:

1. _____ ☐
2. _____ ☐
3. _____ ☐
4. _____ ☐
5. _____ ☐

Inspired Actions:

Today's Lessons and Insights:

> *"There is no failure except in no longer trying."*
>
> ~ *Elbert Hubbard*

Tuesday

Date: _____

Intentions for Today:

Daily Habits:

Visualize Goals as Complete	AM ☐	PM ☐
Say Affirmations for Goals	AM ☐	PM ☐
Express Appreciation/Gratitude	Self ☐	Someone Else ☐

Meditate ☐ Notes: _____

Read ☐ Notes: _____

Exercise ☐ Notes: _____

"Letting Go" ☐ Method: _____

Journal ☐ Notes: _____

Optional Habit ☐ Notes: _____

Five Daily Planned Actions:

1. _____ ☐

2. _____ ☐

3. _____ ☐

4. _____ ☐

5. _____ ☐

Inspired Actions:

Today's Lessons and Insights:

Fun fact: *Being too serious can ruin your success; it can create extra problems and obstacles such as stress, anxiety, and emotional pain.*

Wednesday

Date: _____

Intentions for Today:

Daily Habits:

Visualize Goals as Complete	AM ☐	PM ☐
Say Affirmations for Goals	AM ☐	PM ☐
Express Appreciation/Gratitude	Self ☐	Someone Else ☐

Meditate ☐ Notes: _____

Read ☐ Notes: _____

Exercise ☐ Notes: _____

"Letting Go" ☐ Method: _____

Journal ☐ Notes: _____

Optional Habit ☐ Notes: _____

Five Daily Planned Actions:

1. _____ ☐
2. _____ ☐
3. _____ ☐
4. _____ ☐
5. _____ ☐

Inspired Actions:

Today's Lessons and Insights:

> *"A wise man will make more opportunities than he finds."*
>
> ~ *Francis Bacon*

Thursday   Date: _____

Intentions for Today:

Daily Habits:

Visualize Goals as Complete	AM ☐	PM ☐
Say Affirmations for Goals	AM ☐	PM ☐
Express Appreciation/Gratitude	Self ☐	Someone Else ☐

Meditate ☐ Notes: _____

Read ☐ Notes: _____

Exercise ☐ Notes: _____

"Letting Go" ☐ Method: _____

Journal ☐ Notes: _____

Optional Habit ☐ Notes: _____

Five Daily Planned Actions:

1. _____ ☐

2. _____ ☐

3. _____ ☐

4. _____ ☐

5. _____ ☐

Inspired Actions:

Today's Lessons and Insights:

> **Tip of the week:** *Set at least one breakthrough goal. Think of what would really change the game for you and rocket you forward.*

Friday

Date: _____

Intentions for Today:

Daily Habits:

Visualize Goals as Complete	AM ☐	PM ☐
Say Affirmations for Goals	AM ☐	PM ☐
Express Appreciation/Gratitude	Self ☐	Someone Else ☐

Meditate ☐ Notes: _____

Read ☐ Notes: _____

Exercise ☐ Notes: _____

"Letting Go" ☐ Method: _____

Journal ☐ Notes: _____

Optional Habit ☐ Notes: _____

Five Daily Planned Actions:

1. _____ ☐

2. _____ ☐

3. _____ ☐

4. _____ ☐

5. _____ ☐

Inspired Actions:

Today's Lessons and Insights:

"To achieve happiness, we should make certain that we are never without an important goal."
~ Earl Nightingale

Saturday

Date: _____

Intentions for Today:

Daily Habits:

Visualize Goals as Complete	AM ☐	PM ☐
Say Affirmations for Goals	AM ☐	PM ☐
Express Appreciation/Gratitude	Self ☐	Someone Else ☐

Meditate ☐ Notes: _____

Read ☐ Notes: _____

Exercise ☐ Notes: _____

"Letting Go" ☐ Method: _____

Journal ☐ Notes: _____

Optional Habit ☐ Notes: _____

Five Daily Planned Actions:

1. _____ ☐

2. _____ ☐

3. _____ ☐

4. _____ ☐

5. _____ ☐

Inspired Actions:

Today's Lessons and Insights:

Powerful success resources: *Think and Grow Rich by Napoleon Hill. This classic has stood the test of time and is worth rereading frequently.*

Sunday

Date: _____

Intentions for Today:

Daily Habits:

Visualize Goals as Complete	AM ☐	PM ☐
Say Affirmations for Goals	AM ☐	PM ☐
Express Appreciation/Gratitude	Self ☐	Someone Else ☐

Meditate ☐ Notes: _____

Read ☐ Notes: _____

Exercise ☐ Notes: _____

"Letting Go" ☐ Method: _____

Journal ☐ Notes: _____

Optional Habit ☐ Notes: _____

Five Daily Planned Actions:

1. _____ ☐

2. _____ ☐

3. _____ ☐

4. _____ ☐

5. _____ ☐

Inspired Actions:

Today's Lessons and Insights:

"When you get an intuitive hit, follow it quickly even if you don't fully understand it. To ignore that gift will stop more from coming." ~ Pete Winiarski

Weekly Summary

Week 5

Tally of Last Week's Check Marks:

Daily Habits:

Visualize Goals as Complete	_____ / 14
Say Affirmations for Goals	_____ / 14
Appreciation/ Gratitude	_____ / 14
Meditate	_____ / 7
Read	_____ / 7
Exercise	_____ / 7
"Letting Go"	_____ / 7
Journal	_____ / 7
Optional Habit	_____ / 7
Five Daily Actions:	_____ / 35

This Week's Total Score

Out of 119

Last Week's Insights:

Next Week's Goals:

> **Challenge of the week:** *Send a note of appreciation and gratitude to a different person every day this week.*

Monday

Date: _____

Intentions for Today:

Daily Habits:

Visualize Goals as Complete	AM ☐	PM ☐
Say Affirmations for Goals	AM ☐	PM ☐
Express Appreciation/Gratitude	Self ☐	Someone Else ☐

Meditate ☐ Notes: _____

Read ☐ Notes: _____

Exercise ☐ Notes: _____

"Letting Go" ☐ Method: _____

Journal ☐ Notes: _____

Optional Habit ☐ Notes: _____

Five Daily Planned Actions:

1. _____ ☐

2. _____ ☐

3. _____ ☐

4. _____ ☐

5. _____ ☐

Inspired Actions:

Today's Lessons and Insights:

> *"Failure teaches success."*
>
> ~ *Japanese proverb*

Tuesday   Date: _____

Intentions for Today:

Daily Habits:

Visualize Goals as Complete	AM ☐	PM ☐
Say Affirmations for Goals	AM ☐	PM ☐
Express Appreciation/Gratitude	Self ☐	Someone Else ☐

Meditate ☐ Notes: _____

Read ☐ Notes: _____

Exercise ☐ Notes: _____

"Letting Go" ☐ Method: _____

Journal ☐ Notes: _____

Optional Habit ☐ Notes: _____

Five Daily Planned Actions:

1. _____ ☐

2. _____ ☐

3. _____ ☐

4. _____ ☐

5. _____ ☐

Inspired Actions:

Today's Lessons and Insights:

Fun fact: *Michael Jordon has been trusted to take the game-winning shot and missed twenty-six times. Overall he has missed nine thousand shots in his career and lost almost three hundred games.*

Wednesday

Date: _____

Intentions for Today:

Daily Habits:

Visualize Goals as Complete	AM ☐	PM ☐
Say Affirmations for Goals	AM ☐	PM ☐
Express Appreciation/Gratitude	Self ☐	Someone Else ☐

Meditate ☐ Notes: _____

Read ☐ Notes: _____

Exercise ☐ Notes: _____

"Letting Go" ☐ Method: _____

Journal ☐ Notes: _____

Optional Habit ☐ Notes: _____

Five Daily Planned Actions:

1. _____ ☐

2. _____ ☐

3. _____ ☐

4. _____ ☐

5. _____ ☐

Inspired Actions:

Today's Lessons and Insights:

"The great and glorious masterpiece of man is to know how to live to purpose."
~ *Michel de Montaigne*

Thursday

Date: _____

Intentions for Today:

Daily Habits:

Visualize Goals as Complete	AM ☐	PM ☐
Say Affirmations for Goals	AM ☐	PM ☐
Express Appreciation/Gratitude	Self ☐	Someone Else ☐

Meditate ☐ Notes: _____

Read ☐ Notes: _____

Exercise ☐ Notes: _____

"Letting Go" ☐ Method: _____

Journal ☐ Notes: _____

Optional Habit ☐ Notes: _____

Five Daily Planned Actions:

1. _____ ☐

2. _____ ☐

3. _____ ☐

4. _____ ☐

5. _____ ☐

Inspired Actions:

Today's Lessons and Insights:

Tip of the week: *Celebrate every win, big and small.*

Friday

Date: _____

Intentions for Today:

Daily Habits:

Visualize Goals as Complete	AM ☐	PM ☐
Say Affirmations for Goals	AM ☐	PM ☐
Express Appreciation/Gratitude	Self ☐	Someone Else ☐

Meditate ☐ Notes: _____

Read ☐ Notes: _____

Exercise ☐ Notes: _____

"Letting Go" ☐ Method: _____

Journal ☐ Notes: _____

Optional Habit ☐ Notes: _____

Five Daily Planned Actions:

1. _____ ☐

2. _____ ☐

3. _____ ☐

4. _____ ☐

5. _____ ☐

Inspired Actions:

Today's Lessons and Insights:

> *"What you get by achieving your goals is as important as what you become by achieving your goals."*
> ~ *Henry David Thoreau*

Saturday

Date: _____

Intentions for Today:

Daily Habits:

Visualize Goals as Complete	AM ☐	PM ☐
Say Affirmations for Goals	AM ☐	PM ☐
Express Appreciation/Gratitude	Self ☐	Someone Else ☐

Meditate ☐ Notes: _____

Read ☐ Notes: _____

Exercise ☐ Notes: _____

"Letting Go" ☐ Method: _____

Journal ☐ Notes: _____

Optional Habit ☐ Notes: _____

Five Daily Planned Actions:

1. _____ ☐

2. _____ ☐

3. _____ ☐

4. _____ ☐

5. _____ ☐

Inspired Actions:

Today's Lessons and Insights:

Powerful success resources: *Dear God Letter,* www.DearGodLetter.com *is a powerful goal accelerator.*

Sunday

Date: _____

Intentions for Today:

Daily Habits:

Visualize Goals as Complete	AM ☐	PM ☐
Say Affirmations for Goals	AM ☐	PM ☐
Express Appreciation/Gratitude	Self ☐	Someone Else ☐

Meditate ☐ Notes: _____

Read ☐ Notes: _____

Exercise ☐ Notes: _____

"Letting Go" ☐ Method: _____

Journal ☐ Notes: _____

Optional Habit ☐ Notes: _____

Five Daily Planned Actions:

1. _____ ☐

2. _____ ☐

3. _____ ☐

4. _____ ☐

5. _____ ☐

Inspired Actions:

Today's Lessons and Insights:

> *"Focus on your strengths and leverage them to bigger success. Understand your weaknesses and leverage other people on your team to manage them for you."*
> ~ Pete Winiarski

Weekly Summary   Week 6

Tally of Last Week's Check Marks:

Daily Habits:

Visualize Goals as Complete	_____ / 14	
Say Affirmations for Goals	_____ / 14	
Appreciation/ Gratitude	_____ / 14	
Meditate	_____ / 7	
Read	_____ / 7	
Exercise	_____ / 7	
"Letting Go"	_____ / 7	
Journal	_____ / 7	
Optional Habit	_____ / 7	
Five Daily Actions:	_____ / 35	

This Week's Total Score

Out of 119

Last Week's Insights:

_____

_____

_____

_____

_____

Next Week's Goals:

_____

_____

_____

_____

_____

Monday

Date: _____

Intentions for Today:

Daily Habits:

Visualize Goals as Complete	AM ☐	PM ☐
Say Affirmations for Goals	AM ☐	PM ☐
Express Appreciation/Gratitude	Self ☐	Someone Else ☐

Meditate ☐ Notes: _____

Read ☐ Notes: _____

Exercise ☐ Notes: _____

"Letting Go" ☐ Method: _____

Journal ☐ Notes: _____

Optional Habit ☐ Notes: _____

Five Daily Planned Actions:

1. _____ ☐

2. _____ ☐

3. _____ ☐

4. _____ ☐

5. _____ ☐

Inspired Actions:

Today's Lessons and Insights:

"The surest way not to fail is to determine to succeed."

~ *Richard Brinsley Sheridan*

Tuesday

Date: _____

Intentions for Today:

Daily Habits:

Visualize Goals as Complete	AM ☐	PM ☐
Say Affirmations for Goals	AM ☐	PM ☐
Express Appreciation/Gratitude	Self ☐	Someone Else ☐

Meditate ☐ Notes: _____

Read ☐ Notes: _____

Exercise ☐ Notes: _____

"Letting Go" ☐ Method: _____

Journal ☐ Notes: _____

Optional Habit ☐ Notes: _____

Five Daily Planned Actions:

1. _____ ☐

2. _____ ☐

3. _____ ☐

4. _____ ☐

5. _____ ☐

Inspired Actions:

Today's Lessons and Insights:

> **Fun fact:** *Abraham Lincoln and Winston Churchill both lost multiple elections for public office before eventually becoming president and prime minister (respectively).*

Wednesday
Date: _____

Intentions for Today:

Daily Habits:

Visualize Goals as Complete	AM ☐	PM ☐
Say Affirmations for Goals	AM ☐	PM ☐
Express Appreciation/Gratitude	Self ☐	Someone Else ☐

Meditate ☐ Notes: _____

Read ☐ Notes: _____

Exercise ☐ Notes: _____

"Letting Go" ☐ Method: _____

Journal ☐ Notes: _____

Optional Habit ☐ Notes: _____

Five Daily Planned Actions:

1. _____ ☐
2. _____ ☐
3. _____ ☐
4. _____ ☐
5. _____ ☐

Inspired Actions:

Today's Lessons and Insights:

> *"Nothing can stop the man with the right mental attitude from achieving his goal; nothing on earth can help the man with the wrong mental attitude."*   ~ *Thomas Jefferson*

Thursday

Date: _____

Intentions for Today:

Daily Habits:

Visualize Goals as Complete	AM ☐ PM ☐
Say Affirmations for Goals	AM ☐ PM ☐
Express Appreciation/Gratitude	Self ☐ Someone Else ☐

Meditate ☐ Notes: _____

Read ☐ Notes: _____

Exercise ☐ Notes: _____

"Letting Go" ☐ Method: _____

Journal ☐ Notes: _____

Optional Habit ☐ Notes: _____

Five Daily Planned Actions:

1. _____ ☐

2. _____ ☐

3. _____ ☐

4. _____ ☐

5. _____ ☐

Inspired Actions:

Today's Lessons and Insights:

Tip of the week: *Ask for help. Success is a team sport.*

Friday

Date: _____

Intentions for Today:

Daily Habits:

Visualize Goals as Complete	AM ☐	PM ☐
Say Affirmations for Goals	AM ☐	PM ☐
Express Appreciation/Gratitude	Self ☐	Someone Else ☐

Meditate ☐ Notes: _____

Read ☐ Notes: _____

Exercise ☐ Notes: _____

"Letting Go" ☐ Method: _____

Journal ☐ Notes: _____

Optional Habit ☐ Notes: _____

Five Daily Planned Actions:

1. _____ ☐

2. _____ ☐

3. _____ ☐

4. _____ ☐

5. _____ ☐

Inspired Actions:

Today's Lessons and Insights:

> *"Our goals can only be reached through a vehicle of a plan, in which we must fervently be-*
> *lieve, and upon which we must vigorously act."* ~ *Vincent van Gogh*

Saturday

Date: _____

Intentions for Today:

Daily Habits:

Visualize Goals as Complete	AM ☐ PM ☐
Say Affirmations for Goals	AM ☐ PM ☐
Express Appreciation/Gratitude	Self ☐ Someone Else ☐

Meditate ☐ Notes: _____

Read ☐ Notes: _____

Exercise ☐ Notes: _____

"Letting Go" ☐ Method: _____

Journal ☐ Notes: _____

Optional Habit ☐ Notes: _____

Five Daily Planned Actions:

1. _____ ☐

2. _____ ☐

3. _____ ☐

4. _____ ☐

5. _____ ☐

Inspired Actions:

Today's Lessons and Insights:

> **Powerful success resources:** *The Passion Test by Janet Bray Attwood and Chris Attwood.*

Sunday

Date: _____

Intentions for Today:

Daily Habits:

Visualize Goals as Complete	AM ☐	PM ☐
Say Affirmations for Goals	AM ☐	PM ☐
Express Appreciation/Gratitude	Self ☐	Someone Else ☐

Meditate ☐ Notes: _____

Read ☐ Notes: _____

Exercise ☐ Notes: _____

"Letting Go" ☐ Method: _____

Journal ☐ Notes: _____

Optional Habit ☐ Notes: _____

Five Daily Planned Actions:

1. _____ ☐

2. _____ ☐

3. _____ ☐

4. _____ ☐

5. _____ ☐

Inspired Actions:

Today's Lessons and Insights:

> *"Practice what I call The Napoleon Hill Formula: C+B=A. As Napoleon Hill has taught us, what the mind can Conceive and Believe it can Achieve."*　　*~ Pete Winiarski*

Weekly Summary　　　　Week 7

Tally of Last Week's Check Marks:

Daily Habits:

Visualize Goals as Complete	_____ / 14	
Say Affirmations for Goals	_____ / 14	
Appreciation/ Gratitude	_____ / 14	
Meditate	_____ / 7	
Read	_____ / 7	
Exercise	_____ / 7	
"Letting Go"	_____ / 7	
Journal	_____ / 7	
Optional Habit	_____ / 7	
Five Daily Actions:	_____ / 35	

This Week's Total Score

Out of 119

Last Week's Insights:

_____

_____

_____

_____

_____

Next Week's Goals:

_____

_____

_____

_____

_____

> **Challenge of the week:** *Set your alarm an hour earlier than normal every day this week to get a head start on your day.*

Monday

Date: _____

Intentions for Today:

Daily Habits:

Visualize Goals as Complete	AM ☐	PM ☐
Say Affirmations for Goals	AM ☐	PM ☐
Express Appreciation/Gratitude	Self ☐	Someone Else ☐

Meditate	☐	Notes: _____
Read	☐	Notes: _____
Exercise	☐	Notes: _____
"Letting Go"	☐	Method: _____
Journal	☐	Notes: _____
Optional Habit	☐	Notes: _____

Five Daily Planned Actions:

1. _____ ☐
2. _____ ☐
3. _____ ☐
4. _____ ☐
5. _____ ☐

Inspired Actions:

Today's Lessons and Insights:

> *"To reach a port we must sail, sometimes with the wind and sometimes against it. But we must not drift or lie at anchor."*   *~ Oliver Wendell Holmes, Sr.*

Tuesday   Date: _____

Intentions for Today:

Daily Habits:

Visualize Goals as Complete	AM ☐	PM ☐
Say Affirmations for Goals	AM ☐	PM ☐
Express Appreciation/Gratitude	Self ☐	Someone Else ☐

Meditate ☐ Notes: _____

Read ☐ Notes: _____

Exercise ☐ Notes: _____

"Letting Go" ☐ Method: _____

Journal ☐ Notes: _____

Optional Habit ☐ Notes: _____

Five Daily Planned Actions:

1. _____ ☐
2. _____ ☐
3. _____ ☐
4. _____ ☐
5. _____ ☐

Inspired Actions:

Today's Lessons and Insights:

Fun fact: *Thomas Edison had over a thousand failed attempts at creating the light bulb before finally creating the model that changed the modern world.*

Wednesday   Date: _____

Intentions for Today:

Daily Habits:

Visualize Goals as Complete	AM ☐ PM ☐
Say Affirmations for Goals	AM ☐ PM ☐
Express Appreciation/Gratitude	Self ☐ Someone Else ☐

Meditate ☐ Notes: _____

Read ☐ Notes: _____

Exercise ☐ Notes: _____

"Letting Go" ☐ Method: _____

Journal ☐ Notes: _____

Optional Habit ☐ Notes: _____

Five Daily Planned Actions:

1. _____ ☐

2. _____ ☐

3. _____ ☐

4. _____ ☐

5. _____ ☐

Inspired Actions:

Today's Lessons and Insights:

"It is hard to fail, but it is worse never to have tried to succeed."

~ *Theodore Roosevelt*

Thursday

Date: _____

Intentions for Today:

Daily Habits:

Visualize Goals as Complete   AM ☐   PM ☐

Say Affirmations for Goals   AM ☐   PM ☐

Express Appreciation/Gratitude   Self ☐   Someone Else ☐

Meditate   ☐   Notes: _____

Read   ☐   Notes: _____

Exercise   ☐   Notes: _____

"Letting Go"   ☐   Method: _____

Journal   ☐   Notes: _____

Optional Habit   ☐   Notes: _____

Five Daily Planned Actions:

1. _____ ☐

2. _____ ☐

3. _____ ☐

4. _____ ☐

5. _____ ☐

Inspired Actions:

Today's Lessons and Insights:

Friday

Date: _____

Intentions for Today:

Daily Habits:

Visualize Goals as Complete	AM ☐	PM ☐
Say Affirmations for Goals	AM ☐	PM ☐
Express Appreciation/Gratitude	Self ☐	Someone Else ☐

Meditate ☐ Notes: _____

Read ☐ Notes: _____

Exercise ☐ Notes: _____

"Letting Go" ☐ Method: _____

Journal ☐ Notes: _____

Optional Habit ☐ Notes: _____

Five Daily Planned Actions:

1. _____ ☐

2. _____ ☐

3. _____ ☐

4. _____ ☐

5. _____ ☐

Inspired Actions:

Today's Lessons and Insights:

> *"Don't be too timid and squeamish about your actions. All life is an experiment. The more experiments you make the better."*
> ~ *Ralph Waldo Emerson*

Saturday

Date: _____

Intentions for Today:

Daily Habits:

Visualize Goals as Complete	AM ☐	PM ☐
Say Affirmations for Goals	AM ☐	PM ☐
Express Appreciation/Gratitude	Self ☐	Someone Else ☐

Meditate ☐ Notes: _____

Read ☐ Notes: _____

Exercise ☐ Notes: _____

"Letting Go" ☐ Method: _____

Journal ☐ Notes: _____

Optional Habit ☐ Notes: _____

Five Daily Planned Actions:

1. _____ ☐
2. _____ ☐
3. _____ ☐
4. _____ ☐
5. _____ ☐

Inspired Actions:

Today's Lessons and Insights:

Sunday

Date: _____

Intentions for Today:

Daily Habits:

Visualize Goals as Complete	AM ☐	PM ☐
Say Affirmations for Goals	AM ☐	PM ☐
Express Appreciation/Gratitude	Self ☐	Someone Else ☐

Meditate ☐ Notes: _____

Read ☐ Notes: _____

Exercise ☐ Notes: _____

"Letting Go" ☐ Method: _____

Journal ☐ Notes: _____

Optional Habit ☐ Notes: _____

Five Daily Planned Actions:

1. _____ ☐

2. _____ ☐

3. _____ ☐

4. _____ ☐

5. _____ ☐

Inspired Actions:

Today's Lessons and Insights:

Weekly Summary   Week 8

Tally of Last Week's Check Marks:

Daily Habits:

Visualize Goals as Complete	_____ / 14
Say Affirmations for Goals	_____ / 14
Appreciation/ Gratitude	_____ / 14
Meditate	_____ / 7
Read	_____ / 7
Exercise	_____ / 7
"Letting Go"	_____ / 7
Journal	_____ / 7
Optional Habit	_____ / 7
Five Daily Actions:	_____ / 35

This Week's Total Score

Out of 119

Last Week's Insights:

_____

_____

_____

_____

_____

Next Week's Goals:

_____

_____

_____

_____

_____

> **Challenge of the week:** *Try a new method of "Letting Go" this week, and consciously practice it on an issue every day.*

Monday

Date: _____

Intentions for Today:

Daily Habits:

Visualize Goals as Complete	AM ☐	PM ☐
Say Affirmations for Goals	AM ☐	PM ☐
Express Appreciation/Gratitude	Self ☐	Someone Else ☐

Meditate ☐ Notes: _____

Read ☐ Notes: _____

Exercise ☐ Notes: _____

"Letting Go" ☐ Method: _____

Journal ☐ Notes: _____

Optional Habit ☐ Notes: _____

Five Daily Planned Actions:

1. _____ ☐

2. _____ ☐

3. _____ ☐

4. _____ ☐

5. _____ ☐

Inspired Actions:

Today's Lessons and Insights:

"The secret of achievement is to hold a picture of a successful outcome in the mind."
~ Henry David Thoreau

Tuesday
Date: _____

Intentions for Today:

Daily Habits:

Visualize Goals as Complete	AM ☐	PM ☐
Say Affirmations for Goals	AM ☐	PM ☐
Express Appreciation/Gratitude	Self ☐	Someone Else ☐

Meditate ☐ Notes: _____

Read ☐ Notes: _____

Exercise ☐ Notes: _____

"Letting Go" ☐ Method: _____

Journal ☐ Notes: _____

Optional Habit ☐ Notes: _____

Five Daily Planned Actions:

1. _____ ☐
2. _____ ☐
3. _____ ☐
4. _____ ☐
5. _____ ☐

Inspired Actions:

Today's Lessons and Insights:

Wednesday

Date: _____

Intentions for Today:

Daily Habits:

Visualize Goals as Complete	AM ☐	PM ☐
Say Affirmations for Goals	AM ☐	PM ☐
Express Appreciation/Gratitude	Self ☐	Someone Else ☐

Meditate ☐ Notes: _____

Read ☐ Notes: _____

Exercise ☐ Notes: _____

"Letting Go" ☐ Method: _____

Journal ☐ Notes: _____

Optional Habit ☐ Notes: _____

Five Daily Planned Actions:

1. _____ ☐

2. _____ ☐

3. _____ ☐

4. _____ ☐

5. _____ ☐

Inspired Actions:

Today's Lessons and Insights:

> *"To climb steep hills requires a slow pace at first."*
>
> ~ *William Shakespeare*

Thursday

Date: _____

Intentions for Today:

Daily Habits:

Visualize Goals as Complete	AM ☐ PM ☐
Say Affirmations for Goals	AM ☐ PM ☐
Express Appreciation/Gratitude	Self ☐ Someone Else ☐

Meditate ☐ Notes: _____

Read ☐ Notes: _____

Exercise ☐ Notes: _____

"Letting Go" ☐ Method: _____

Journal ☐ Notes: _____

Optional Habit ☐ Notes: _____

Five Daily Planned Actions:

1. _____ ☐

2. _____ ☐

3. _____ ☐

4. _____ ☐

5. _____ ☐

Inspired Actions:

Today's Lessons and Insights:

Tip of the week: *Schedule time in your calendar for your goal-related actions.*

Friday

Date: _____

Intentions for Today:

Daily Habits:

Visualize Goals as Complete	AM ☐	PM ☐
Say Affirmations for Goals	AM ☐	PM ☐
Express Appreciation/Gratitude	Self ☐	Someone Else ☐

Meditate ☐ Notes: _____

Read ☐ Notes: _____

Exercise ☐ Notes: _____

"Letting Go" ☐ Method: _____

Journal ☐ Notes: _____

Optional Habit ☐ Notes: _____

Five Daily Planned Actions:

1. _____ ☐

2. _____ ☐

3. _____ ☐

4. _____ ☐

5. _____ ☐

Inspired Actions:

Today's Lessons and Insights:

> *"What is not started today is never finished tomorrow."*
> ~ *Johann Wolfgang von Goethe*

Saturday

Date: _____

Intentions for Today:

Daily Habits:

Visualize Goals as Complete	AM ☐	PM ☐
Say Affirmations for Goals	AM ☐	PM ☐
Express Appreciation/Gratitude	Self ☐	Someone Else ☐

Meditate ☐ Notes: _____

Read ☐ Notes: _____

Exercise ☐ Notes: _____

"Letting Go" ☐ Method: _____

Journal ☐ Notes: _____

Optional Habit ☐ Notes: _____

Five Daily Planned Actions:

1. _____ ☐
2. _____ ☐
3. _____ ☐
4. _____ ☐
5. _____ ☐

Inspired Actions:

Today's Lessons and Insights:

Sunday

Date: _____

Intentions for Today:

Daily Habits:

Visualize Goals as Complete	AM ☐	PM ☐
Say Affirmations for Goals	AM ☐	PM ☐
Express Appreciation/Gratitude	Self ☐	Someone Else ☐

Meditate ☐ Notes: _____

Read ☐ Notes: _____

Exercise ☐ Notes: _____

"Letting Go" ☐ Method: _____

Journal ☐ Notes: _____

Optional Habit ☐ Notes: _____

Five Daily Planned Actions:

1. _____ ☐

2. _____ ☐

3. _____ ☐

4. _____ ☐

5. _____ ☐

Inspired Actions:

Today's Lessons and Insights:

> *"As you achieve your goal, take time to celebrate—that celebration builds 'muscle memory' and helps your next goal come even easier."*
> ~ *Pete Winiarski*

Weekly Summary   Week 9

Tally of Last Week's Check Marks:

Daily Habits:

Visualize Goals as Complete	_____ / 14	
Say Affirmations for Goals	_____ / 14	
Appreciation/ Gratitude	_____ / 14	
Meditate	_____ / 7	
Read	_____ / 7	
Exercise	_____ / 7	
"Letting Go"	_____ / 7	
Journal	_____ / 7	
Optional Habit	_____ / 7	
Five Daily Actions:	_____ / 35	

This Week's Total Score

[ ]

Out of 119

Last Week's Insights:

_____

_____

_____

_____

_____

Next Week's Goals:

_____

_____

_____

_____

_____

> **Challenge of the week:** *Every evening this week before bed, look in the mirror and tell yourself how much you appreciate your efforts.*

Monday

Date: _____

Intentions for Today:

Daily Habits:

Visualize Goals as Complete	AM ☐	PM ☐
Say Affirmations for Goals	AM ☐	PM ☐
Express Appreciation/Gratitude	Self ☐	Someone Else ☐

Meditate ☐ Notes: _____

Read ☐ Notes: _____

Exercise ☐ Notes: _____

"Letting Go" ☐ Method: _____

Journal ☐ Notes: _____

Optional Habit ☐ Notes: _____

Five Daily Planned Actions:

1. _____ ☐
2. _____ ☐
3. _____ ☐
4. _____ ☐
5. _____ ☐

Inspired Actions:

Today's Lessons and Insights:

"Have regular hours for work and play; make each day both useful and pleasant, and prove that you understand the worth of time by employing it well." ~ Louisa May Alcott

Tuesday

Date: _____

Intentions for Today:

Daily Habits:

Visualize Goals as Complete	AM ☐	PM ☐
Say Affirmations for Goals	AM ☐	PM ☐
Express Appreciation/Gratitude	Self ☐	Someone Else ☐

Meditate ☐ Notes: _____

Read ☐ Notes: _____

Exercise ☐ Notes: _____

"Letting Go" ☐ Method: _____

Journal ☐ Notes: _____

Optional Habit ☐ Notes: _____

Five Daily Planned Actions:

1. _____ ☐

2. _____ ☐

3. _____ ☐

4. _____ ☐

5. _____ ☐

Inspired Actions:

Today's Lessons and Insights:

> **Fun fact:** *Emotionally charged goals have a much higher likelihood of becoming reality than ones that are created without any excitement behind them.*

Wednesday

Date: _____

Intentions for Today:

Daily Habits:

Visualize Goals as Complete	AM ☐	PM ☐
Say Affirmations for Goals	AM ☐	PM ☐
Express Appreciation/Gratitude	Self ☐	Someone Else ☐

Meditate ☐ Notes: _____

Read ☐ Notes: _____

Exercise ☐ Notes: _____

"Letting Go" ☐ Method: _____

Journal ☐ Notes: _____

Optional Habit ☐ Notes: _____

Five Daily Planned Actions:

1. _____ ☐
2. _____ ☐
3. _____ ☐
4. _____ ☐
5. _____ ☐

Inspired Actions:

Today's Lessons and Insights:

> *"The greater danger for most of us lies not in setting our aim too high and falling short; but in setting our aim too low, and achieving our mark."*
> ~ Michelangelo

Thursday

Date: _____

Intentions for Today:

Daily Habits:

Visualize Goals as Complete   AM ☐ PM ☐

Say Affirmations for Goals   AM ☐ PM ☐

Express Appreciation/Gratitude Self ☐ Someone Else ☐

Meditate ☐ Notes: _____

Read   ☐ Notes: _____

Exercise ☐ Notes: _____

"Letting Go" ☐ Method: _____

Journal   ☐ Notes: _____

Optional Habit ☐ Notes: _____

Five Daily Planned Actions:

1. _____ ☐

2. _____ ☐

3. _____ ☐

4. _____ ☐

5. _____ ☐

Inspired Actions:

Today's Lessons and Insights:

Tip of the week: *Start your day with one of the daily habits rather than squeeze it in later.*

Friday

Date: _____

Intentions for Today:

Daily Habits:

Visualize Goals as Complete	AM ☐	PM ☐
Say Affirmations for Goals	AM ☐	PM ☐
Express Appreciation/Gratitude	Self ☐	Someone Else ☐

Meditate ☐ Notes: _____

Read ☐ Notes: _____

Exercise ☐ Notes: _____

"Letting Go" ☐ Method: _____

Journal ☐ Notes: _____

Optional Habit ☐ Notes: _____

Five Daily Planned Actions:

1. _____ ☐
2. _____ ☐
3. _____ ☐
4. _____ ☐
5. _____ ☐

Inspired Actions:

Today's Lessons and Insights:

> *"When it is obvious that the goals cannot be reached, don't adjust the goals, adjust the action steps."*
> ~ Confucius

Saturday   Date: _____

Intentions for Today:

Daily Habits:

Visualize Goals as Complete	AM ☐	PM ☐
Say Affirmations for Goals	AM ☐	PM ☐
Express Appreciation/Gratitude	Self ☐	Someone Else ☐

Meditate ☐ Notes: _____

Read ☐ Notes: _____

Exercise ☐ Notes: _____

"Letting Go" ☐ Method: _____

Journal ☐ Notes: _____

Optional Habit ☐ Notes: _____

Five Daily Planned Actions:

1. _____ ☐
2. _____ ☐
3. _____ ☐
4. _____ ☐
5. _____ ☐

Inspired Actions:

Today's Lessons and Insights:

Powerful success resources: *The Institute of HeartMath,*
www.HeartMathInfo.com.

Sunday

Date: _____

Intentions for Today:

Daily Habits:

Visualize Goals as Complete   AM ☐   PM ☐

Say Affirmations for Goals   AM ☐   PM ☐

Express Appreciation/Gratitude   Self ☐   Someone Else ☐

Meditate   ☐   Notes: _____

Read   ☐   Notes: _____

Exercise   ☐   Notes: _____

"Letting Go"   ☐   Method: _____

Journal   ☐   Notes: _____

Optional Habit   ☐   Notes: _____

Five Daily Planned Actions:

1. _____   ☐

2. _____   ☐

3. _____   ☐

4. _____   ☐

5. _____   ☐

Inspired Actions:

Today's Lessons and Insights:

> *"Look forward with enthusiasm, rather than be discouraged; trust that where you are right now is where you are supposed to be."*
>
> *~ Pete Winiarski*

Weekly Summary Week 10

Tally of Last Week's Check Marks:

Daily Habits:

Visualize Goals as Complete	_____ / 14	
Say Affirmations for Goals	_____ / 14	
Appreciation/ Gratitude	_____ / 14	
Meditate	_____ / 7	
Read	_____ / 7	
Exercise	_____ / 7	
"Letting Go"	_____ / 7	
Journal	_____ / 7	
Optional Habit	_____ / 7	
Five Daily Actions:	_____ / 35	

This Week's Total Score

Out of 119

Last Week's Insights:

_____

_____

_____

_____

_____

Next Week's Goals:

_____

_____

_____

_____

_____

Challenge of the week: *Choose at least one book to read cover to cover this week.*

Monday

Date: _____

Intentions for Today:

Daily Habits:

Visualize Goals as Complete	AM ☐	PM ☐
Say Affirmations for Goals	AM ☐	PM ☐
Express Appreciation/Gratitude	Self ☐	Someone Else ☐

Meditate ☐ Notes: _____

Read ☐ Notes: _____

Exercise ☐ Notes: _____

"Letting Go" ☐ Method: _____

Journal ☐ Notes: _____

Optional Habit ☐ Notes: _____

Five Daily Planned Actions:

1. _____ ☐

2. _____ ☐

3. _____ ☐

4. _____ ☐

5. _____ ☐

Inspired Actions:

Today's Lessons and Insights:

> *"What would life be if we had no courage to attempt anything?"*
>
> ~ *Vincent van Gogh*

Tuesday   Date: _____

Intentions for Today:

Daily Habits:

Visualize Goals as Complete	AM ☐	PM ☐
Say Affirmations for Goals	AM ☐	PM ☐
Express Appreciation/Gratitude	Self ☐	Someone Else ☐

Meditate ☐ Notes: _____

Read ☐ Notes: _____

Exercise ☐ Notes: _____

"Letting Go" ☐ Method: _____

Journal ☐ Notes: _____

Optional Habit ☐ Notes: _____

Five Daily Planned Actions:

1. _____ ☐

2. _____ ☐

3. _____ ☐

4. _____ ☐

5. _____ ☐

Inspired Actions:

Today's Lessons and Insights:

Wednesday

Date: _____

Intentions for Today:

Daily Habits:

Visualize Goals as Complete	AM ☐	PM ☐
Say Affirmations for Goals	AM ☐	PM ☐
Express Appreciation/Gratitude	Self ☐	Someone Else ☐

Meditate ☐ Notes: _____

Read ☐ Notes: _____

Exercise ☐ Notes: _____

"Letting Go" ☐ Method: _____

Journal ☐ Notes: _____

Optional Habit ☐ Notes: _____

Five Daily Planned Actions:

1. _____ ☐

2. _____ ☐

3. _____ ☐

4. _____ ☐

5. _____ ☐

Inspired Actions:

Today's Lessons and Insights:

> *"The talent of success is nothing more than doing what you can do, well."*
> ~ *Henry W. Longfellow*

Thursday

Date: _____

Intentions for Today:

Daily Habits:

Visualize Goals as Complete	AM ☐	PM ☐
Say Affirmations for Goals	AM ☐	PM ☐
Express Appreciation/Gratitude	Self ☐	Someone Else ☐

Meditate ☐ Notes: _____

Read ☐ Notes: _____

Exercise ☐ Notes: _____

"Letting Go" ☐ Method: _____

Journal ☐ Notes: _____

Optional Habit ☐ Notes: _____

Five Daily Planned Actions:

1. _____ ☐

2. _____ ☐

3. _____ ☐

4. _____ ☐

5. _____ ☐

Inspired Actions:

Today's Lessons and Insights:

Friday

Date: _____

Intentions for Today:

Daily Habits:

Visualize Goals as Complete	AM ☐	PM ☐
Say Affirmations for Goals	AM ☐	PM ☐
Express Appreciation/Gratitude	Self ☐	Someone Else ☐

Meditate ☐ Notes: _____

Read ☐ Notes: _____

Exercise ☐ Notes: _____

"Letting Go" ☐ Method: _____

Journal ☐ Notes: _____

Optional Habit ☐ Notes: _____

Five Daily Planned Actions:

1. _____ ☐
2. _____ ☐
3. _____ ☐
4. _____ ☐
5. _____ ☐

Inspired Actions:

Today's Lessons and Insights:

> *"Don't judge each day by the harvest you reap but by the seeds that you plant."*
> *~ Robert Louis Stevenson*

Saturday

Date: _____

Intentions for Today:

Daily Habits:

Visualize Goals as Complete	AM ☐	PM ☐
Say Affirmations for Goals	AM ☐	PM ☐
Express Appreciation/Gratitude	Self ☐	Someone Else ☐

Meditate ☐ Notes: _____

Read ☐ Notes: _____

Exercise ☐ Notes: _____

"Letting Go" ☐ Method: _____

Journal ☐ Notes: _____

Optional Habit ☐ Notes: _____

Five Daily Planned Actions:

1. _____ ☐
2. _____ ☐
3. _____ ☐
4. _____ ☐
5. _____ ☐

Inspired Actions:

Today's Lessons and Insights:

Sunday

Date: _____

Intentions for Today:

Daily Habits:

Visualize Goals as Complete	AM ☐	PM ☐
Say Affirmations for Goals	AM ☐	PM ☐
Express Appreciation/Gratitude	Self ☐	Someone Else ☐

Meditate	☐	Notes: _____
Read	☐	Notes: _____
Exercise	☐	Notes: _____
"Letting Go"	☐	Method: _____
Journal	☐	Notes: _____
Optional Habit	☐	Notes: _____

Five Daily Planned Actions:

1. _____ ☐
2. _____ ☐
3. _____ ☐
4. _____ ☐
5. _____ ☐

Inspired Actions:

Today's Lessons and Insights:

> *"Magic seems to happen when I'm conscious about appreciating others and feeling grateful for all I have already."*
> *~ Pete Winiarski*

Weekly Summary   Week 11

Tally of Last Week's Check Marks:

Daily Habits:

Visualize Goals as Complete	_____ / 14
Say Affirmations for Goals	_____ / 14
Appreciation/ Gratitude	_____ / 14
Meditate	_____ / 7
Read	_____ / 7
Exercise	_____ / 7
"Letting Go"	_____ / 7
Journal	_____ / 7
Optional Habit	_____ / 7
Five Daily Actions:	_____ / 35

This Week's Total Score

Out of 119

Last Week's Insights:

_____
_____
_____
_____
_____

Next Week's Goals:

_____
_____
_____
_____
_____

> **Challenge of the week:** *Eliminate television from your life every day this week (yes, including the weekend) and replace that time with action on your goals.*

Monday   Date: _____

Intentions for Today:

Daily Habits:

Visualize Goals as Complete   AM ☐   PM ☐

Say Affirmations for Goals   AM ☐   PM ☐

Express Appreciation/Gratitude   Self ☐   Someone Else ☐

Meditate ☐   Notes: _____

Read ☐   Notes: _____

Exercise ☐   Notes: _____

"Letting Go" ☐   Method: _____

Journal ☐   Notes: _____

Optional Habit ☐   Notes: _____

Five Daily Planned Actions:

1. _____ ☐

2. _____ ☐

3. _____ ☐

4. _____ ☐

5. _____ ☐

Inspired Actions:

Today's Lessons and Insights:

> *"The greatest mistake you can make in life is to continually be afraid you will make one."*
> *~ Elbert Hubbard*

Tuesday

Date: _____

Intentions for Today:

Daily Habits:

Visualize Goals as Complete	AM ☐	PM ☐
Say Affirmations for Goals	AM ☐	PM ☐
Express Appreciation/Gratitude	Self ☐	Someone Else ☐

Meditate ☐ Notes: _____

Read ☐ Notes: _____

Exercise ☐ Notes: _____

"Letting Go" ☐ Method: _____

Journal ☐ Notes: _____

Optional Habit ☐ Notes: _____

Five Daily Planned Actions:

1. _____ ☐

2. _____ ☐

3. _____ ☐

4. _____ ☐

5. _____ ☐

Inspired Actions:

Today's Lessons and Insights:

> *Fun fact:* Goal achievement spurs happiness, but it can also eventually bring about boredom. In order to continue feeling happy, it is important to always create more goals.

Wednesday   Date: _____

Intentions for Today:

Daily Habits:

Visualize Goals as Complete	AM ☐	PM ☐
Say Affirmations for Goals	AM ☐	PM ☐
Express Appreciation/Gratitude	Self ☐	Someone Else ☐

Meditate ☐ Notes: _____

Read ☐ Notes: _____

Exercise ☐ Notes: _____

"Letting Go" ☐ Method: _____

Journal ☐ Notes: _____

Optional Habit ☐ Notes: _____

Five Daily Planned Actions:

1. _____ ☐

2. _____ ☐

3. _____ ☐

4. _____ ☐

5. _____ ☐

Inspired Actions:

Today's Lessons and Insights:

> *"Excellence is not an act but a habit"*
>
> ~ *Aristotle*

Thursday

Date: _____

Intentions for Today:

Daily Habits:

Visualize Goals as Complete	AM ☐	PM ☐
Say Affirmations for Goals	AM ☐	PM ☐
Express Appreciation/Gratitude	Self ☐	Someone Else ☐

Meditate ☐ Notes: _____

Read ☐ Notes: _____

Exercise ☐ Notes: _____

"Letting Go" ☐ Method: _____

Journal ☐ Notes: _____

Optional Habit ☐ Notes: _____

Five Daily Planned Actions:

1. _____ ☐

2. _____ ☐

3. _____ ☐

4. _____ ☐

5. _____ ☐

Inspired Actions:

Today's Lessons and Insights:

Friday

Date: _____

Intentions for Today:

Daily Habits:

Visualize Goals as Complete	AM ☐	PM ☐
Say Affirmations for Goals	AM ☐	PM ☐
Express Appreciation/Gratitude	Self ☐	Someone Else ☐

Meditate ☐ Notes: _____

Read ☐ Notes: _____

Exercise ☐ Notes: _____

"Letting Go" ☐ Method: _____

Journal ☐ Notes: _____

Optional Habit ☐ Notes: _____

Five Daily Planned Actions:

1. _____ ☐

2. _____ ☐

3. _____ ☐

4. _____ ☐

5. _____ ☐

Inspired Actions:

Today's Lessons and Insights:

> *"An idea not coupled with action will never get any bigger than the brain cell it occupied."*
> ~ *Arnold H. Glasow*

Saturday

Date: _____

Intentions for Today:

Daily Habits:

Visualize Goals as Complete	AM ☐ PM ☐
Say Affirmations for Goals	AM ☐ PM ☐
Express Appreciation/Gratitude	Self ☐ Someone Else ☐

Meditate	☐	Notes: _____
Read	☐	Notes: _____
Exercise	☐	Notes: _____
"Letting Go"	☐	Method: _____
Journal	☐	Notes: _____
Optional Habit	☐	Notes: _____

Five Daily Planned Actions:

1. _____ ☐
2. _____ ☐
3. _____ ☐
4. _____ ☐
5. _____ ☐

Inspired Actions:

Today's Lessons and Insights:

Powerful success resources: *The Secret by Rhonda Byrne will help you understand the law of attraction.*

Sunday

Date: _____

Intentions for Today:

Daily Habits:

Visualize Goals as Complete   AM ☐   PM ☐

Say Affirmations for Goals   AM ☐   PM ☐

Express Appreciation/Gratitude   Self ☐   Someone Else ☐

Meditate   ☐   Notes: _____

Read   ☐   Notes: _____

Exercise   ☐   Notes: _____

"Letting Go"   ☐   Method: _____

Journal   ☐   Notes: _____

Optional Habit   ☐   Notes: _____

Five Daily Planned Actions:

1. _____ ☐

2. _____ ☐

3. _____ ☐

4. _____ ☐

5. _____ ☐

Inspired Actions:

Today's Lessons and Insights:

"If you believe that anything is possible, is there any reason to limit yourself?"

~ Pete Winiarski

Weekly Summary   Week 12

Tally of Last Week's Check Marks:

Daily Habits:

Visualize Goals as Complete	_____ / 14
Say Affirmations for Goals	_____ / 14
Appreciation/ Gratitude	_____ / 14
Meditate	_____ / 7
Read	_____ / 7
Exercise	_____ / 7
"Letting Go"	_____ / 7
Journal	_____ / 7
Optional Habit	_____ / 7
Five Daily Actions:	_____ / 35

This Week's Total Score

Out of 119

Last Week's Insights:

_____

_____

_____

_____

_____

Next Week's Goals:

_____

_____

_____

_____

_____

Challenge of the week: *Find at least one success to celebrate this week, and include other people in your celebration—let them know about your success.*

Monday

Date: _____

Intentions for Today:

Daily Habits:

Visualize Goals as Complete	AM ☐	PM ☐
Say Affirmations for Goals	AM ☐	PM ☐
Express Appreciation/Gratitude	Self ☐	Someone Else ☐

Meditate ☐ Notes: _____

Read ☐ Notes: _____

Exercise ☐ Notes: _____

"Letting Go" ☐ Method: _____

Journal ☐ Notes: _____

Optional Habit ☐ Notes: _____

Five Daily Planned Actions:

1. _____ ☐
2. _____ ☐
3. _____ ☐
4. _____ ☐
5. _____ ☐

Inspired Actions:

Today's Lessons and Insights:

> *"Always bear in mind that your own resolution to succeed is more important than any other one thing."*
> ~ *Abraham Lincoln*

Tuesday

Date: _____

Intentions for Today:

Daily Habits:

Visualize Goals as Complete	AM ☐	PM ☐
Say Affirmations for Goals	AM ☐	PM ☐
Express Appreciation/Gratitude	Self ☐	Someone Else ☐

Meditate ☐ Notes: _____

Read ☐ Notes: _____

Exercise ☐ Notes: _____

"Letting Go" ☐ Method: _____

Journal ☐ Notes: _____

Optional Habit ☐ Notes: _____

Five Daily Planned Actions:

1. _____ ☐
2. _____ ☐
3. _____ ☐
4. _____ ☐
5. _____ ☐

Inspired Actions:

Today's Lessons and Insights:

Fun fact: *By making a conscious effort to not listen to any form of constant negativity, you can cut a significant amount of stress and anxiety in your life.*

Wednesday   Date: _____

Intentions for Today:

Daily Habits:

Visualize Goals as Complete	AM ☐	PM ☐
Say Affirmations for Goals	AM ☐	PM ☐
Express Appreciation/Gratitude	Self ☐	Someone Else ☐

Meditate ☐ Notes: _____

Read ☐ Notes: _____

Exercise ☐ Notes: _____

"Letting Go" ☐ Method: _____

Journal ☐ Notes: _____

Optional Habit ☐ Notes: _____

Five Daily Planned Actions:

1. _____ ☐

2. _____ ☐

3. _____ ☐

4. _____ ☐

5. _____ ☐

Inspired Actions:

Today's Lessons and Insights:

"Energy and persistence conquer all things."

~ *Benjamin Franklin*

Thursday

Date: _____

Intentions for Today:

Daily Habits:

Visualize Goals as Complete	AM ☐	PM ☐
Say Affirmations for Goals	AM ☐	PM ☐
Express Appreciation/Gratitude	Self ☐	Someone Else ☐

Meditate ☐ Notes: _____

Read ☐ Notes: _____

Exercise ☐ Notes: _____

"Letting Go" ☐ Method: _____

Journal ☐ Notes: _____

Optional Habit ☐ Notes: _____

Five Daily Planned Actions:

1. _____ ☐

2. _____ ☐

3. _____ ☐

4. _____ ☐

5. _____ ☐

Inspired Actions:

Today's Lessons and Insights:

Friday

Date: _____

Intentions for Today:

Daily Habits:

Visualize Goals as Complete   AM ☐   PM ☐

Say Affirmations for Goals   AM ☐   PM ☐

Express Appreciation/Gratitude   Self ☐   Someone Else ☐

Meditate   ☐   Notes: _____

Read   ☐   Notes: _____

Exercise   ☐   Notes: _____

"Letting Go"   ☐   Method: _____

Journal   ☐   Notes: _____

Optional Habit   ☐   Notes: _____

Five Daily Planned Actions:

1. _____ ☐

2. _____ ☐

3. _____ ☐

4. _____ ☐

5. _____ ☐

Inspired Actions:

Today's Lessons and Insights:

> *"Gratitude is the best attitude."*
>
> ~ *Author unknown*

Saturday

Date: _____

Intentions for Today:

Daily Habits:

Visualize Goals as Complete	AM ☐	PM ☐
Say Affirmations for Goals	AM ☐	PM ☐
Express Appreciation/Gratitude	Self ☐	Someone Else ☐

Meditate ☐ Notes: _____

Read ☐ Notes: _____

Exercise ☐ Notes: _____

"Letting Go" ☐ Method: _____

Journal ☐ Notes: _____

Optional Habit ☐ Notes: _____

Five Daily Planned Actions:

1. _____ ☐

2. _____ ☐

3. _____ ☐

4. _____ ☐

5. _____ ☐

Inspired Actions:

Today's Lessons and Insights:

Powerful success resources: *Powerful meditations at Win Conscious Leadership, www.WinConsciousLeadership.com*

Sunday

Date: _____

Intentions for Today:

Daily Habits:

Visualize Goals as Complete	AM ☐ PM ☐
Say Affirmations for Goals	AM ☐ PM ☐
Express Appreciation/Gratitude	Self ☐ Someone Else ☐

Meditate	☐	Notes: _____
Read	☐	Notes: _____
Exercise	☐	Notes: _____
"Letting Go"	☐	Method: _____
Journal	☐	Notes: _____
Optional Habit	☐	Notes: _____

Five Daily Planned Actions:

1. _____ ☐
2. _____ ☐
3. _____ ☐
4. _____ ☐
5. _____ ☐

Inspired Actions:

Today's Lessons and Insights:

> *"If it's true that a predictor of your success is the success levels of the people you spend the most time with, are you willing to spend your time differently?"*   ~ Pete Winiarski

Weekly Summary   Week 13

Tally of Last Week's Check Marks:

Daily Habits:

Visualize Goals as Complete	_____ / 14	
Say Affirmations for Goals	_____ / 14	
Appreciation/ Gratitude	_____ / 14	**This Week's Total Score**
Meditate	_____ / 7	
Read	_____ / 7	
Exercise	_____ / 7	
"Letting Go"	_____ / 7	
Journal	_____ / 7	**Out of 119**
Optional Habit	_____ / 7	
Five Daily Actions:	_____ / 35	

Last Week's Insights:

_____

_____

_____

_____

_____

Next Week's Goals:

_____

_____

_____

_____

_____

Invitation

I invite you to download copies of the worksheets used in this book and other free resources you will find helpful along your goal achieving journey. There are also a number of resources I described throughout the book. For easy reference, I've placed a master list on the website for you, too. Visit www.DailyActionLog.com.

Also, please read and comment about the latest blog posting. Visit www.DailyActionBlog.com.

Acknowledgments

My beautiful wife, Marie: Thank you for being amazing and for your unending support for all my projects and ideas. Your love, encouragement, and excitement keeps me energized.

Nicholas and Nathan: Thank you for helping me relive my childhood and for visiting me in my office every day when you get home from school. I enjoy your stories and love hearing you describe why today was so amazing for you.

Kelly Bluestein and Jennifer Acheson: Wow! Without you I'd be far from finished with this book and dozens of other projects. You have created typed pages out of my bumpy chicken scratch from my working on airplanes. You pushed me when I needed to get things done so you could take the next step. You adjusted your schedules around my travelling so we could work on things in the office together. You are both important players on the Win Team—I appreciate your dedication. Thank you!

Jack Canfield: thank you for being a supportive mentor and friend. I am especially grateful that you took the time to write the foreword; I know how busy you are. You managed to capture your thoughts about *Act Now!* masterfully. Many of these daily habits I learned from you. This book would not have been written were it not for BTS, TTT, and the community you created. The initial idea to write this book was born during TTT and here it is—all by taking action! I appreciate you!

Patty Aubrey: You are amazing, as always. You turned my initial concept into something bigger and more complete. Your probing questions helped me clarify my direction and ensure this book is aligned with my consulting work. I value your vision and your heart equally. You are a special person.

Sam Holomua Chillingworth, Alice Doughty, Andrea Haefele, Jesse Ianniello, all of the staff at Jack's office, and the other assistants at Jack's trainings: I'm glad we can make each other laugh. Thank you for your genuine love and support. You are among my closest friends and supporters.

Tracy Gulden: Thanks for some fast action logo/graphics work. You always manage to put pictures to our words.

My two mastermind teams: Your detailed feedback and marketing ideas helped make this book much, much better. Kym Belden, Holly Carnes, Louie Sharp, Sean Smith, Sharon Worsley: thank you for the steady flow of ideas which helped clarify my thinking and approach for the book and website. Leland Brandt, Alan Nathan, and Bruce Stanger: I enjoy our breakfast discussions. You helped this book (and all my business ideas) take off. Thank you all.

Sean Smith: I especially want to thank you for your guidance in teaching me NLP and in understanding our unconscious minds better. This content supports an important section of the book. We've also had many memorable and enjoyable conversations. You are a true friend.

Kim Mylls: Thank you for asking me each morning on our way to Jack's training, "What's your intention for today?" That is a powerful part of this book. Also, thanks for helping me realize that thousands of people are building their network marketing businesses and need this book, too. You are a strong leader with great insights. Thanks for always being there.

Deirdre Hade: Your coaching and encouragement helped me remember how important this book really is. Thank you for sharing your light.

Chris Goralski: Your insight about placing the goals chapter first was priceless and made a big difference in the final version.

Kathy Hanford: I enjoyed our discussions about fitting this type of work in the corporate environment. Thank you for the vote of confidence.

To all the other company presidents and executives who reviewed the early draft of the manuscript and offered suggestions from the perspective of business leaders: Thank you for taking the time out of your busy schedules.

To the many others who shared their thoughts about the manuscript, marketing, website, or other ideas to help make *Act Now!* a success: Thank you.

Kay Balbi and Jeanine Longfritz: I want to especially acknowledge you for sharing your extensive notes and edits to the entire manuscript. Your thoughts were so useful.

To all my friends and clients who used some earlier variation of the methods that became *Act Now!*: Thank you for sharing your thoughts and helping me determine what works best for you.

Last, I owe a special thank you to the team at CreateSpace. You have made the process easy and are great partners for us here at Win Publishing.

About the Author

Pete Winiarski is the founder and president of Win Enterprises, LLC. He has over two decades of experience in corporate leadership and consulting roles.

In addition to leading his company, Pete is a highly skilled results coach and speaker. He is a lifelong student of the Science of Success, an avid reader, and applies what he has learned in his work. Pete has been mentored by Jack Canfield and assists at Jack's training. This is Pete's second book.

For more information, please visit www.PeteWiniarski.com.

About Win Enterprises, LLC

Win Enterprises, LLC is a firm that helps business leaders achieve and sustain transformational results. Win's approach, summarized in the Win Holistic Transformation Model™, is heavily influenced by the Science of Success, Strategic Goal Deployment™, Lean Thinking, Conscious Leadership, and creating a Winning Team. This model also recognizes the importance of shifting company cultures to sustain the results you achieve. *Act Now!* can help you shift your company culture to become more action orientated and focused on your most important goals.

Contact Win Enterprises to help you solve your business problems and transform your results with:

- Business consulting
- Results coaching
- Keynote speaking
- Workshops

Visit www.WinEnterprisesLLC.com for the full story.

Get Additional Help

For help using the principles in this book, please visit www.DailyActionLog.com.

For help transforming your business or personal results, and to engage Win Enterprises in consulting or coaching, contact our office directly.

To invite Pete Winiarski to speak at your event, contact our office directly.

Office contact:

Telephone: 860-651-6859
Email: info@WinEnterprisesLLC.com.

Bibliography

Books

Attwood, Janet Bray, and Chris Attwood. *The Passion Test*. New York: Penguin, 2006.

Byrne, Rhonda. *The Secret*. New York: Simon & Schuster, Inc., 2006.

Canfield, Jack, Mark Victor, and Les Hewitt, *The Power of Focus*. Deerfield Beach: Health Communications, Inc., 2000.

Canfield, Jack. *The Success Principles*. New York: HarperCollins Publishers, Inc., 2005.

Dwoskin, Hale. *The Sedona Method*, 7–8. Sedona: Sedona Press, 2007.

Eker, T. Harv. *Secrets of the Millionaire Mind: Mastering the Inner Game of Wealth*. New York: HarperCollins, 2005.

Emmons, Robert, A. *Thanks! How the New Science of Gratitude Can Make You Happier*. Boston: Houghton Mifflin Company, 2007.

Ferriss, Timothy. *The 4-Hour Work Week: Escape 9-5, Live Anywhere, and Join the New Rich*. New York: Crown Publishers, 2007.

George, Bill, and Peter Sims. *True North: Discover your Authentic Leadership*. San Francisco: Jossey-Bass, 2007.

Hill, Napoleon. *Think and Grow Rich*, 197–198. New York: Penguin Group, 2005.

Lipton, Bruce H. *The Biology of Belief*. New York: Hay House, Inc., 2008.

McTaggart, Lynne. *The Field*. New York: HarperCollins, 2002.

McTaggart, Lynne. *The Intention Experiment*. New York: Free Press, 2007.

Random House. *The Random House College Dictionary*, 693. New York: Random House, 1982.

Ready, Romilla, and Kate Burton. *Neuro-linguistic Programming for Dummies*, 18. New Jersey: John Wiley & Sons, 2004.

Sharma, Robin. *The Leader Who Had No Title*. New York: Free Press, 2010.

Vitale, Joe, and Ihaleakala Hew Len. *Zero Limits*. New Jersey: John Wiley & Sons, 2007.

Audio Products

Canfield, Jack and Deborah Sandella. *Awakening Power: A Step-by-Step Guided Visualization Program Guaranteed to Activate "The Secret" in Your Life*. Jack Canfield and Deborah Sandella, The Canfield Training Group, 2008.

Evans, Richard Paul. *Capturing Million Dollar Ideas: Discovering the Power of Idea Journaling*. Book Wise, 2008.

Hade, Deirdre Hade. *Radiance: Pure Energy*. Learning Strategies Corp., 2011.

Mali, Jeddah. *Seeds of Enlightenment*. Learning Strategies Corp., 2008.

Peterson, Tiffany Walke. *Sales Mastery with Tiffany Peterson: Discover the Secrets, Skills, and Systems to Succeed in Sales*. T. Peterson, 2011.

Smith, Sean. *Emotional Mastery: How to Achieve Absolute Control of Your Thoughts, Feeling and Beliefs*. MVP Success Systems, 2010.

Smith, Sean. *Releasing the Brakes: How to Eliminate All Your Fears and Limiting Beliefs*. MVP Success Systems, 2010.

Seminars and Training

Canfield Training Group, PO Box 30880, Santa Barbara, CA 93130: www.JackCanfieldInfo.com.

Sedona Training Associates, 60 Tortilla Drive, Sedona, AZ 86336: www.TheSedonaMethodInfo.com. The Sedona Method is a powerful tool for self-improvement and spiritual growth by "Letting Go."

Articles/Special Reports/Websites

Barrett, Deirdre. *Answers in Your Dreams. Scientific American Mind*, November/December 2011.

Belyea, Jeff. *Meditation In The Corporate Boardroom.* www.selfgrowth.com/ articles/Meditation_In_The_Corporate_Boardroom.html. 2008.

Cameron, Julia. *Morning Pages.* www.JuliaCameronLive.com/basic-tools/morning-pages/. 2012.

Childre, Doc. *HeartMath.* www.HeartMathInfo.com. 1991.

Isaac, Brad. *The 26 Major Advantages to Reading More Books and Why 3 in 4 People Are Being Shut Out of Success.* 2007.

Oddo, Tiffany and Pete Winiarski. *Myths & Misconceptions about Meditation.* 2010.

Wenner, Janns. *Rolling Stone, The Beatles' 100 Greatest Songs.* November 2010.

Quotes

Permission given by Sean Smith

Permission given by Ann-McGee Cooper

Permission given by Tiffany Peterson

Permission given by Jack Canfield

All other quotes remain intellectual property of their respective originators. We do not assert any claim of copyright for individual quotations. All use of quotations is done under the "fair use" copyright principle.

Notes
(Endnotes)

1   Dr. Gail Matthews, Goals Research Summary. Submitted for publication as of October 12, 2011. http://www.dominican.edu/academics/ahss/psych/faculty/full-time/gailmatthews/researchsummary2.pdf

2   Random House, *The Random House College Dictionary* (New York: Random House, 1982), 693.

3   The Institute of Heartmath, www.heartmath.org.

4   Lynne McTaggart, *The Field* (New York: HarperCollins Publishers, 2002).

5   Tiffany Oddo, and Pete Winiarski. Myths & Misconceptions About Meditation, http://www.AwakenYourConsciousness.com, 3

6   Jeff Belyea. "Meditation in the Corporate Boardroom". April 15, 2008. http://www.selfgrowth.com/articles/Meditation_In_The_Corporate_Boardroom.html.

7   Ricardo Lumbardo. Meditation Power— Understanding How it Works. http://ezinearticles.com/?Meditation-Power---Understanding-How-It-Works&id=4981837.

8   Oliver Ryan. *CNN Money*. "How to Succeed in Business: Meditate," July 20, 2007. http://money.cnn.com/magazines/fortune/fortune_archive/2007/07/23/100135590/index.htm.

9   Nadja Brandt. "Wall Street Bosses, Tiger Woods Meditate to Focus, Stay Calm," October 22, 2008. http://www.bloomberg.com/apps/news?pid=newsarchive&sid=aR2aP.X_Bflw

10   Brad Isaac. "The 26 Major Advantages to Reading More books and Why 3 in 4 People Are Being Shut Out of Success," December 5, 2007. www.PersistenceUnlimited.com

11   Hale Dwoskin. *The Sedona Method* (Sedona: Sedona Press, 2007), 7–8.

12   Jack Canfield. *The Success Principles* (New York: HarperCollins Publishers, Inc., 2005), 178.

13   Jann S. Wenner. *Rolling Stone*, "The Beatles' 100 Greatest Songs," November 2010, 18.

14   Deirdre Barrett. "Answers in Your Dreams," *Scientific American Mind*, November/December 2011, 18.

15   Napoleon Hill. *Think and Grow Rich* (New York: Penguin Group, 2005), 197–198.

16   Dr. Gail Matthews, Goals Research Summary. Submitted for publication as of October 12, 2011. http://www.dominican.edu/academics/ahss/psych/faculty/full-time/gailmatthews/researchsummary2.pdf.

Please Share Act Now! and Introduce Us

We know the *Act Now!* methodology can help lots of people, but we don't personally know them all. We need your help to introduce them to us. Most of our business contacts come from personal introductions and referrals. Will you help us spread the word?

We'd love to send you two signed copies of *Act Now!* when you make an introduction to someone who hires us as a keynote speaker, to conduct a workshop for their team, or to coach them through the *Act Now!* methodology.

Email us at info@WinEnterprisesLLC.com to make an introduction.